YOU AND YOUR MONEY

MAKING SENSE OF PERSONAL FINANCE

HENRY E. RIGGS

To order additional copies of this book, contact:
Xlibris Corporation
1-888-795-4274
www.Xlibris.com
Orders@Xlibris.com
122190

Dedicated to

Sarah, Christopher, Carson, Molly, Sam, and Gretchen

Special thanks to Carson Witte for his outstanding editing
help, bringing to bear the viewpoint of a target reader!

Thanks also to Gayle Riggs, Eleanor Mansfield, Linda Elkind,
and Catharine Riggs for their continuing advice.

Table of Contents

Preface

This book addresses the very many considerations people face in handling their income and savings, investing, borrowing, protecting against risks, and tax planning.

Somewhat surprisingly, our educational system, at the high school level and beyond, rarely addresses this myriad of issues—both problems and opportunities—that can be categorized as personal finances. Our schools lecture ceaselessly about the challenges of drugs, sex, alcohol, smoking, social media, and wellness—and appropriately so, since young people are exposed to endless opportunities to make poor and harmful decisions regarding each of those matters.

But so also are adults at all ages—teenagers to senior citizens—confronted by a host of challenges and opportunities as to how to manage their personal finances—from before they receive their first paychecks and continuing on through retirement and death. As we proceed through high school, college, and even graduate school, we may take courses in accounting, finance, economics, and taxation, all of which offer tidbits of advice on handling our personal finances, but none are comprehensive in addressing personal finance. This book seeks to fill that void.

We are bombarded with information, suggestions, inducements, promises, threats, and political dialogue that relate to our financial well-being. This bombardment comes primarily from individuals and companies that have a stake in getting us to enter into a financial arrangement with them (e.g., banks, lawyers, securities brokers, life-insurance agents, lenders—including auto, appliance, and other retailers—and real estate brokers). Many of these—in fact, most—are subject to some governmental regulations that restrict them from outright lying. But regulators are hard-pressed to fashion requirements that would result in full and unbiased disclosure of benefits, costs, and risks associated with various financial decisions. Sellers of financial products and services will inevitably, and understandably, emphasize benefits more than risks, even as they meet the requirements for disclosure of both.

The result, *caveat emptor*—buyer beware.

This book seeks to increase your awareness of financial matters. Here are some questions (issues) discussed:

- Your monthly credit card statement prominently states your "minimum required payment." Does this imply that paying the minimum, rather than the full balance, is prudent?
- Every retail bank window advertises CD rates (certificate of deposit interest rates) offered by the bank. Do these ads make clear what penalty will be levied on the savings if you must "cash in" the CD before maturity? Do they imply that CDs are the wisest savings vehicle?
- Auto dealerships advertise, during slow periods, interest rates on auto loans as low as 0 percent. Does any organization really lend money without charging interest?
- Life insurance advertising suggests that a whole-life policy (what does that phrase mean?) will not only protect your family but also build a retirement nest egg for you. Is such a policy the financially efficient way to achieve these dual objectives?
- A particular mutual fund has racked up outstanding performance over the past year. Regulations require the fine print at the bottom of its advertising to point out that "past performance is no guarantee of future performance," but should a potential investor focus primarily on those funds with recent stellar records?
- Should the owner of a bond be pleased or disappointed when she reads that "prevailing interest rates" (whatever that phrase means) have recently increased?

Scan the newspapers or the Internet, or listen to radio and TV broadcasts of financial news. Many terms used in financial reports are mysterious or unintentionally misleading.

- What is an index? Why do so many of them exist, and are some more reliable or meaningful than others?
- Is a stock that sells for $23 per share a better "value" than another that sells for $47 per share?
- Should you be drawn to or be wary of a high "yield" or a low "multiple" stock?
- A particular security has a high "outstanding short position." What does that mean, and should you care if you are considering buying or selling that security?
- You see that the bonds of a particular company have over the past seven years achieved a nominal return of 7 percent but a "real" return of 3 percent. What's the difference? More fundamentally, what is a bond?
- The Securities and Exchange Commission (SEC) has approved the initial public offering (IPO) of a company headquartered in your city. Does the SEC thereby endorse the common shares being offered by this company?

- Another company has "cut its dividend." What does that mean, and does that action imply you should consider buying or selling the securities of that company?
- Yet another company is about to sell preferred stock. "Preferred" sounds better than "common." What are the risks and benefits of owning one rather than the other?
- Around tax time each year (that is, the weeks leading up to April 15), references are made to "deductions," "tax brackets," "refunds," "earned versus passive income," "quarterly installments," 1099 forms, K-1s, and "qualified dividends," and so forth.
- Every paycheck shows various deductions taken from earnings for this pay period and for the year-to-date. What direct or long-term benefits are financed by these deductions?
- Should employees subscribe to their employer's 401(k) plan even though they are reluctant to authorize additional deductions from their pay?

And the list goes on and on!

The objective of this small volume is to bring together in one place a discussion of the very many issues that face every employed—or soon-to-be employed—citizen in a developed economy such as the United States. Our educational systems focus on literacy and "numeracy" (in addition to much else), as they should. But "financial literacy" is a worthy objective as well, and it is to that objective that this volume is directed.

But be aware that the scope of this book is limited. Its aims do *not* include turning the reader into a Wall Street wonder, a real estate speculator, a bond trader, a life insurance agent, or any of the other financial specialists who populate our world. It should, however, equip the reader to interact productively with these financial experts as he or she considers intelligently a myriad of investment and credit decisions. These decisions typically become more complicated—and more consequential—as a young, well-employed individual's earned income and personal and family responsibilities increase with age and experience. Nonetheless, these days, a young person—long before he or she has gathered any meaningful wealth or even received a single paycheck—is presented the opportunity to make wise or poor financial decisions that can have lingering positive and negative impacts in the years ahead; student loans—borrowing for educational expenses—is a prime example.

I do have an "ax to grind," and I will do some grinding in this small volume. My primary "ax" is inadequate or muddled disclosures by those selling products or services, particularly financial services. For example:

- Some banks charge for the use of debit cards.
- Comparing costs of competing credit card offers is difficult because of extra features or "benefits." Disclosures are extensive, confusing, and difficult to quantify.

- Mortgage lenders may charge the borrower "points" when the mortgage is established and prepayment penalties if the loan is paid down prematurely.

So I will be critical of some of the practices of the many players—individuals and corporations—who populate this very complicated set of markets. Nevertheless, my primary objective is not to describe and vilify a long list of behaviors that I find disappointing, unethical, or, in some cases, bordering on illegal. My purpose is not to "expose" financial misbehaviors, although inevitably, some will be exposed. I will avoid naming names and condemning particular company's practices, even though all examples are—I assure you—drawn from today's financial marketplace.

Instead, my objective is to help educate the customers—that includes all of us—who participate in these markets, sometimes involuntarily and sometimes enthusiastically. I seek to help the reader deal effectively, and for his or her own benefit, with the complex—indeed messy and confusing—financial markets as we now find them, not to reform those markets. (But incidentally, well-informed customers almost always improve the behavior of their "suppliers!")

The financial world—the world of money—is replete with words and phrases that cry out for definition. Throughout this book, these words and phrases are underlined when they first appear and are defined. These "underlinings" are defined in the margin of the page where they first appear; they are also listed in the extensive index at the end of the book.

A few review questions appear at the end of each chapter.

Sprinkled throughout the book are quotes that I hope will be both fun and useful for readers. I begin with one that, as an advice-giving author, I try to bear in mind:

"Advice: a drug on the market, the supply always exceeds the demand."
—Josh Billings

And this preface ends with a quote that defines the book's purpose:

"Chance: that which favors the mind that is prepared."
—Louis Pasteur

Chapter One

INCOME AND NET WORTH

Income: Something you can't live without or within.
　　　　　　　　　　　　—Harry Behmann

I am indeed rich, since my income exceeds my expense,
and my expense is equal of my wishes.
　　　　　　　　　　　　—Edward Gibbon

Salaries and Wages

An individual's primary (but not necessarily sole) source of funds to spend or to save is his or her earned salary. That is, we earn our income in return for expending physical or mental labor. We may be paid by the hour, week, semimonth, or month. From time to time, we may earn bonuses, as a reflection of our own efforts (e.g., sales commissions) or as a reflection of the group's successes (e.g., profit sharing).

Payment almost always comes to us not in cash, but in the form of a check or by direct deposit to our account in a bank or <u>credit union</u>. In advanced economies such as ours in the United States, most purchases and payments are made by check, credit card, or electronically. Still, most of us carry some "walking around money," typically drawn from our accounts through the use of an <u>ATM (automatic teller machine)</u>, for incidental expenses.

The amount of one's paycheck is <u>net earnings</u>—that is, the gross amount earned minus certain <u>deductions</u> mandated by government entities (federal and state taxes of various kinds) or authorized by the wage earner (for medical insurance, a savings plan sponsored by the employer, or other purposes). All

<u>Credit Union:</u> A cooperative group similar to a bank.

<u>ATM:</u> An electronic banking machine that allows customers to make basic transactions without the help of a bank teller.

<u>Net Earnings:</u> The cash one receives by paycheck after all deductions have been taken.

<u>Deductions:</u> Funds taken from one's total earnings for taxes, medical insurance, Social Security, etc.

1

of these data—gross, each deduction, and net—are provided to the earner on each payday. Many people are startled by the magnitude of the difference between gross and net pay.

Internal Revenue Service (IRS): The Federal government's tax collecting agency.

A few more words about these various deductions: The U.S. Internal Revenue Service (IRS) requires employers to deduct an amount from an employee's earnings each pay period; those deductions are typically expected to accumulate over the year to an amount approximating the earner's total income tax obligation for the year. Most states (and some cities) levy income taxes and typically employers are required to deduct amounts for those liabilities as well. Incidentally, employers are required to remit these withheld taxes to the IRS and other taxing authorities on a regular basis; they don't just hold these deducted amounts until the end of the year.

Dependents: The taxpayer's spouse, children, and others whom he or she supports.

Tax Refund: When a taxpayer's pre-payments exceed his final tax liability, the balance is refunded.

The amounts deducted for income taxes are a function of (a) the employee's total expected net earnings for the year, and (b) the number of dependents that the taxpayer supports. Note that these deductions are, in effect, prepayments of the taxpayer's income taxes for which he or she will file a tax return early in the following year. If these payroll tax deductions are likely to total less than the taxpayer's total income tax liability for the year, the taxpayer is required to estimate early in the year what his or her total taxes for the year will be, and then make quarterly prepayments that, together with payroll deductions will add up to the estimated tax liability for the current year.

Filed: Means submitted in tax terms.

Shortfall: The amount by which a taxpayer has underpaid his or her yearly taxes.

If the taxpayer's prepayments and/or payroll tax deductions over the year add up to more than the total tax liability, the difference will be refunded (tax refund) by the IRS soon after the final tax return is filed. If these prepaid taxes fall short of the required amount, the IRS exacts a penalty in addition to the prepayment shortfall.

File Jointly: Husband and wife may calculate and submit their taxes as a couple, rather than individually.

If both husband and wife are wage earners, they may elect to file jointly. Typically, "filing jointly" results in lower total income taxes for the couple than if each "files separately."

Other government tax deductions are mandated by the Federal Insurance Contributions Act (FICA) for programs such as Social Security and Medicare; more on these programs later.

Net Worth of Individuals

Net worth is a phrase more often used in connection with corporations than individuals. Nevertheless, it is a concept or calculation very relevant to the individual's financial planning. An individual's (or a couple's) net worth is simply the difference between what he or she (or they) "owns" (or "own") and "owes" (or "owe")—more formally, the difference between one's assets and one's liabilities. Net worth can be calculated for individuals, couples, families, and organizations such as corporations, schools, religious organizations, and clubs. One important thing to remember is that any error in valuation of an asset or a liability will result in an error in the valuation of net worth, since net worth is, in effect, a derived number. Accurate valuation of an asset or a liability can be much more difficult than it sounds.

The media often refer to an individual's net worth as personal wealth.

Obviously, your earnings, when added to your bank account, increase your net worth and any borrowings you incur reduce your net worth. Expenditures for food, rent, gasoline, and so forth reduce your bank account and your net worth. However, other expenditures change the composition of your net worth but don't reduce it. For example, when you purchase investment securities, a home, a car, or an antique chest, you have just swapped one form of asset for another.

Subsequent chapters explore the implications of credit; that is, borrowing. Suffice to say here that many people have debts that exceed their assets. This condition is particularly prevalent among college students who may be accumulating student loans while they are in school earning little or no income. Obviously, when liabilities exceed assets, an individual's net worth is negative. If the individual had no prospect of income to eventually pay down that debt and thus increase his or her net worth, the individual would be bankrupt (see page 18). Lenders will typically agree to extend additional credit (student loans or credit card borrowing) to individuals with negative net worth *if* they anticipate that the student, following completion of his or her education, will earn a significant income. The lenders will insist on repayment terms that assure orderly debt repayment over a reasonable number of years.

Federal Insurance Contributions Act (FICA): A governmental statute that mandates deductions other than income taxes.

Net Worth: The difference between one's assets and one's liabilities.

Assets: What one owns.

Liabilities: One's financial obligations.

Wealth: Another word for net worth.

Debts: Unpaid obligations, liabilities.

Student Loans: Loans given to people seeking to pursue higher education, who do not yet have a significant income.

An employed individual may also have negative net worth. We know from credit card companies that many persons accumulate large outstanding balances on multiple credit cards—debts they struggle to reduce in light of their current incomes and their on-going household expenses. We will have more to say about this in later chapters; for the moment, we are left to wonder why credit cards companies permit these large build-ups of balances. The simple answer is that the interest rates charged on these large balances are so high that the credit card companies (typically banks) can afford to incur substantial losses on uncollectible balances and still achieve profits on their credit card activities.

Net Worth =

Other Income

Royalties: Money one receives in compensation for the use of one's intellectual and/or creative property—music, books, etc.

Personal income can also arrive in forms other than paychecks. We've already mentioned—and will have more to say about—dividend income and interest income earned on investments. If you lend money to a friend or relative, the interest the borrower pays you is taxable income to you. You might also receive payment for consulting that you do unrelated to your primary job; or royalties on books you have published or musical recordings that you have made; or tips you receive for your personal services such as waiting on tables in a restaurant; or winnings on bets you have made; or payments you receive for renting out a room in your house or lending your pickup truck, and the list goes on. All of these incomes are subject to income tax.

All individuals, regardless of age, are subject to income taxes on monies they earn. If a five-year-old child inherits investment securities from, say, his or her grandparent, future dividends and interest earned by these securities and paid to the child are subject to income tax. A fifteen-year-old who cuts neighborhood lawns earns income that is also subject to income tax. However, our income tax laws exempt a certain nontrivial amount of income from taxation; therefore, most casual income earned by youths does not require any tax payment.

And quite reasonably, gifts are not taxed to the recipient.

Capital Gains

Capital gains earnings are a special case. A capital gain is earned when an asset—a home, an investment security, an artwork piece, an antique car—is sold for a price higher than its cost (referred to as its cost basis), which includes any expenditures that were made to effect improvements in the home or the car, for example. Capital gains are subject to income taxation, but generally at rates lower than those applied to a normal salary income, if the asset had been owned for longer than one year. Accordingly, very large fortunes are more typically accumulated from capital gains than from salary income.

Personal Income Tax Laws and Tax Rates

Taxes: the fine we pay for thriving.

—Anonymous

Personal income tax laws—federal, state, and municipal—are not only very complicated, but are also changed frequently by the relevant governing bodies. The laws and the changes have two major purposes: raising revenue for the government units to spend; and (for federally imposed taxes) influencing taxpayer behavior regarding earning, spending, investing and saving.

For example, when the U.S. Congress sets tax rates for dividend income or capital gains earnings below the rates for so-called earned income, Congress is encouraging taxpayers to invest. When Congress defers taxes on certain retirement savings accounts until the savings are withdrawn to be spent (presumably in retirement), Congress is encouraging savings.

Income taxes are generally graduated by tax brackets. In short, individuals with higher earned income pay both more absolute dollars of income taxes and also a higher percentage of their income as taxes, by comparison to other individuals with lower total earned income. The laws specify the brackets—that is, the relevant salary ranges—and the tax rate that applies to each bracket (see "2012 Tax Brackets" figure).

Capital gains: money earned when an asset is sold for more than it cost to buy and/or improve said asset.

Cost basis: the initial investment in an asset by its owner (i.e. the cost of purchase), as adjusted for alterations made to it during the years it is owned.

Earned Income: Income that is earned through one's physical or mental labor—a salary, as opposed to income earned by selling assets.

Graduated Tax Brackets: Tax rates applicable to increasing (graduated) steps of taxable income

5

Marginal Tax Rate: The rate applicable to the taxpayer's last dollar of taxable income.

Gift Taxes: Taxes owed by a donor who makes gifts to a family members or other individuals that exceed a specified amount per year—currently $13,000—or a specified aggregate amount over his or her lifetime.

Estate Taxes: Applicable when the deceased bequeaths funds to individuals (other than a spouse) exceeding a specified aggregate amount.

A taxpayer's marginal tax rate is the rate at the bracket applicable to his or her last dollar of income. Note that the tax rate on an individual's last dollar of income never exceeds 100 percent; thus, a person who says she cannot afford more income because it will put her in a higher tax bracket is simply talking nonsense!

Lest we forget, individuals are required to pay many taxes that are unrelated to their income: sales taxes, property taxes, vehicle taxes (a part of the annual auto license fee), gasoline taxes, alcohol and tobacco taxes, gift taxes, and estate taxes.

And corporate earnings are taxed at a different schedule of rates. Earnings of a small, unincorporated business are taxed as personal income to the owner(s).

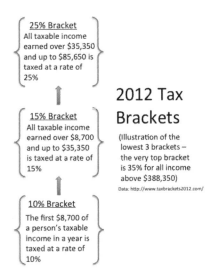

25% Bracket
All taxable income earned over $35,350 and up to $85,650 is taxed at a rate of 25%

2012 Tax Brackets

15% Bracket
All taxable income earned over $8,700 and up to $35,350 is taxed at a rate of 15%

(Illustration of the lowest 3 brackets – the very top bracket is 35% for all income above $388,350)

Data: http://www.taxbrackets2012.com/

10% Bracket
The first $8,700 of a person's taxable income in a year is taxed at a rate of 10%

Allowable Deductions: Deductions made from gross income when calculating the tax to be paid on that income, based on specific qualifiers (such as the presence of dependents) that the taxpayer must meet.

Allowable Deductions

U.S. income tax laws allow you, the taxpayer, specified allowable deductions from gross income that serve to reduce the portion of your income on which you pay taxes (not the actual cash amount of your income). This results in lower taxes. Some of the most significant allowable deductions are:

- An amount for each dependent (children and other individuals who rely on the taxpayer to cover their living expenses.)
- Charitable gifts (subject to some limitations on

amounts) to not-for-profit organizations approved by the taxing authority.
- Medical expenses and medical insurance premiums to the extent they exceed a specified percentage of the taxpayer's income.
- Certain other tax payments, such as state income taxes, taxes on real estate, and personal property taxes.

Tax Reporting

Obviously, failure to report fully and accurately all income received in a year is a serious offense, subject to fines and, in severe cases, imprisonment. As an aside, many criminals are prosecuted for fraudulent tax reporting rather than for their underlying crimes; these criminals fail to report accurately because that accuracy would reveal and highlight their crimes.

The IRS maintains a large staff to <u>audit</u> individual and corporate <u>returns</u> and each audit is typically of several years' returns. In fact, however, only a small percentage of returns ever get audited. The IRS and other taxing authorities have sophisticated computer programs searching within a return for suspicious relationships – for example, moderate income coupled with evidence of a lavish lifestyle. These searches can identify suspicious returns that should be selected for audit.

<u>Audit:</u> The verification by professional accountant of the financial statements of a legal entity.

<u>Returns:</u> Tax reports made by individuals.

A disclaimer: This discussion of taxes (a) is much abbreviated, and (b) seeks to be politically neutral. Alas, one can hardly imagine a topic that is more (a) extensively complicated, and (b) politically charged!

Personal Bankruptcy

A surprising number of individuals have negative net worth: the sum of their outstanding liabilities exceeds the market value of their assets. Nevertheless, these individuals are not necessarily bankrupt. So long as their creditors retain confidence in the individuals' abilities and determination to repay these borrowings more or less on schedule, they will probably not press forward with bankruptcy proceedings.

The subject of bankruptcy is complicated and involves judicial proceedings. A thorough review of the legal processes and outcomes of bankruptcy is beyond the scope of this short volume.

However, two points are worth emphasizing: (a) it is neither illegal nor immoral to become bankrupt or to take the formal, legal step of declaring bankruptcy, and (b) bankruptcy courts generally permit bankrupt individuals to retain certain assets such as clothing and other personal property, a car (to facilitate their remaining or becoming employed), and sometimes even a home. Bankruptcy laws offer protection (from overly aggressive creditors) to those individuals whose debts have grown to such an amount that repayment within a reasonable time frame is very unlikely.

A bankrupt individual—and the management team of a bankrupt corporation (see chapter 5)—carries some stigma, but the circumstances of the bankruptcy influence the extent and the duration of the stigma. An individual entrepreneur who diligently and responsibly pursues a new business opportunity that ultimately proves unsuccessful may find that the damage to his or her business reputation is minimal. On the other hand, a profligate individual who irresponsibly runs up large credit card debt to support a lavish lifestyle, and as a result goes bankrupt, may have great difficulty obtaining loans in the future, and may also suffer from reduced personal and professional respect.

> *Money: not an end in life, but an instrument of life.*
>
> —Henry Ward Beecher

> *Money: a good servant, but a bad master,*
>
> —Henry G. Mohr

Review Questions for Chapter 1:

1. How might an individual come to have negative net worth? Is such an individual bankrupt? Why or why not?
2. What are the primary deductions from a taxpayer's "gross" pay (wages and salaries) that result in a lower "net" taxable income and thus lower tax payments?
3. Not all cash received by an individual is subject to income tax. What are some examples?
4. What set of circumstances might result in a taxpayer receiving a tax refund?

Chapter Two

SAVINGS AND INSURANCE

Abstinence from enjoyment is the only source of wealth.
—Thomas Brassey

Luck: Money in the bank.

—Walter Winchell

Risk Protection

You may be surprised to see the words "savings" and "insurance" linked in the title of this chapter. They are linked because both represent forms of protection against risks.

People accumulate savings to protect against the loss of a job, to pay extra expenses associated with emergencies, and to permit them to retire in reasonable comfort at a target age. Most save for other reasons as well: for the education of their children (or themselves), to accumulate the required <u>down payment</u> for a home, to take a special vacation, or to cover any of a host of other one-time outlays. Many save for no specific foreseen purpose but simply for the peace of mind that comes with having a "nest egg" or "rainy day" fund.

> **Down Payment:** the upfront payment made by a buyer in connection with the purchase of a car, a home, or other expensive item, when borrowing finances the balance of the purchase price.

People purchase insurance for protection against loss or extraordinary costs, for example: loss of property, loss of life, loss of function (i.e., disability), high medical and hospital expenses, and expensive judgments arising from legal proceedings.

Let's consider savings and insurance separately.

Amount of Savings

How much savings should a person have? That is an impossible question to answer in the abstract. Some people don't sleep well if their savings amount to less than a year's worth of expenditures (say, an annual budget amount.) Others are content to spend to (and even beyond) the limits of their income. These are people for whom current consumption of goods and services is so attractive that they are willing to accept the risks associated with emergencies such as illness or the loss of a job.

A prudent and often cited rule of thumb is that one should hold "emergency savings" equal to six-months of expected spending on routine living expenses. However, the appropriate savings amount depends on the circumstances of the individual or family. If the risk of losing a job is relatively high, more accumulated savings might be wise. If the family has generous and comprehensive medical insurance to cover medical emergencies, then lower accumulated savings may be adequate.

A person just entering his or her career will require time to achieve a comfortable savings goal. In addition to the considerations just cited, one's savings goal changes in anticipation of major life events: marriage, the birth of a child, the purchase of a home or its furnishings, remodeling, planned periods of unemployment, or extended travel.

> *Success: The test is simple and infallible. Are you able to save money?*
>
> —James J. Hill

Savings Vehicles

Stuffing cash in a mattress or in the sugar bowl on the top shelf is no way to take care of your savings! Not only are savings handled in these ways subject to theft, these funds produce no earnings.

Return: What one earns from an investment.

Savings need to be invested. Investment alternatives are almost limitless. As a generalization, however, we know that the alternatives offer tradeoffs between return and risk—the greater the potential return, the greater the risk.

The risks are several:

- the risk that the savings will be lost or stolen
- the risk that the savings will not be immediately available in the event of an emergency
- the risk that <u>inflation</u>—that is, increasing prices of goods and services—may outstrip the earnings rate on the savings, causing the savings to lose <u>purchasing power</u>.

The advisable investment vehicle for "emergency savings" is an interest-bearing account. All bank accounts may earn interest. Checking accounts earn a minimal amount, while <u>savings accounts (time deposits)</u> earn a somewhat higher return. Thus, you are advised to separate emergency savings from working balances in your checking account, so that your savings will earn some nontrivial interest. Commercial banks, savings-and-loan banks, and credit unions all offer savings accounts. These accounts are typically guaranteed by the <u>Federal Deposit Insurance Corporation, or FDIC</u>, up to a certain high dollar value in the event the bank or credit union becomes insolvent (i.e., goes broke!). Make sure the institutions you are considering afford you such protection; among those that do, choose the one that offers the highest interest rate on your savings.

<u>Certificates of Deposit (CDs)</u> typically offer higher interest rates than simple savings account deposits, and they too offer the protection of FDIC insurance. However, to earn the advertised CD rate, the saver cannot withdraw any of the invested funds during the term of the CD—generally one, two, or three years. While early withdrawal is possible, it will be accompanied by forfeiture of a significant portion of the accumulated interest. Thus, CDs may be appropriate for only a portion of one's savings: that portion that almost certainly will not be required for emergencies during the term of the CD, or perhaps savings being accumulated for a major future purchase.

Subsequent chapters in this book discuss investment alternatives: fixed-income securities, equity securities (including derivatives), real estate, and commodities. None of these is really appropriate for "emergency savings." They all offer the potential of higher return but with corresponding higher risks, risks that are inappropriate for funds held for emergencies.

<u>Inflation</u>: Loss of value (that is, purchasing power) of money.

<u>Purchasing Power</u>: The market value of a unit of money.

<u>Savings Accounts (time deposits)</u>: Bank accounts on which the depositor earns interest.

<u>FDIC</u>: The Federal government agency that guarantees a bank's deposits in the event the bank fails.

<u>CDs</u>: Savings certificates issued by banks typically providing greater interest returns than bank deposits.

Savings for Retirement

Money is something you got to make in case you don't die.

—Max Asmas

Once fully retired, an employee's regular work-related earnings cease, but living expenses do not. These ongoing expenses are typically met from one or a combination of sources, including: (a) Social Security, (b) pensions, (c) individual retirement accounts (IRAs), (d) annuities, and (e) deferred income contracts. The following paragraphs provide basic information on each of these sources.

Social Security

Social Security Administration:
An agency of the federal government that administers a social insurance program consisting of retirement, disability, and survivors' benefits.

Social Security benefits are paid to retirees (and in some cases, survivors of retirees) by the Social Security Administration. The federal government requires, for virtually all employed wage earners, that monthly payments be made to the Social Security Administration by both the wage-earner (by deduction from his or her earnings) and his or her employer. These payments do *not* go into an account held in trust for the wage-earner; they are simply added to the general pool of funds from which amounts are paid monthly to eligible retirees for the remainder of their lives. These monthly payments reflect the recipient's total earnings from which Social Security deductions have been made over the course of his or her working life. They are subject to periodic "cost-of-living" (inflation) adjustments.

Social Security payments are taxable as ordinary income. Thus, the benefits to recipients in high marginal tax brackets are reduced substantially, as the federal government recoups about one-third of the payment in income taxes collected.

The presumption is that individuals will retire at age sixty-five. Many retire earlier, and their Social Security payments are scaled down accordingly. Those who work past age sixty-five, together with their employers, continue to make payments into the pool, enhancing their future amounts received from Social Security.

As a practical matter, Social Security payments alone will afford the retiree only a very meager postretirement lifestyle. Most retirees need to draw on other funds to maintain their prere-tirement lifestyle. In a moment we will consider the sources of those other funds.

Before leaving the subject of Social Security, however, we should acknowledge that economists and statisticians regularly fore-cast that Social Security will "go broke"—that is, will run out of funds to make its promised distributions to retirees—within twenty to forty years. The reasons are several, but the most im-portant one is that in the eight decades since the Social Security system was started, expected life spans have lengthened sub-stantially. The problem is worse in certain other countries – for example, Japan and Italy – because birth rates in those countries have dropped sharply while years in retirement have grown. Accordingly, with fewer employed people, payments into pro-grams like Social Security decline, while payouts to retirees increase.

Whether the U.S. government will rise to the challenge of "fix-ing" Social Security is problematic. And any affordable "fix" is likely to push the retirement age past sixty-five. In short, Social Security payments are unlikely to return to a level that will alone provide a comfortable retirement.

Pensions: Defined (or Guaranteed) Benefit

Years ago, most employers enrolled their employees in com-pany-sponsored pension plans that assured each employee of retirement income generally geared to the length of time the person was employed by the firm and his or her final salary. Most of these plans were funded: that is, the employer invested sufficient funds, or paid an insurance company, to make the guaranteed payments.

Pension Plans: These plans provide payouts in retirement to former employees of the sponsoring corporation.

In recent decades, funding by many employers has been insuf-ficient and these employers developed what is referred to as an unfunded pension liability. This condition is particularly true for government employers at the state and local level. At the same time, these governments have acceded to the demands of some of their employee groups (e.g., police and firefighters) for earlier retirement and more generous retirement payments. At this point in time it is unclear how these unfunded liabilities will be met, if at all.

Unfunded Pension Liability: Occurs when an employer sets aside insufficient funds to meet a reasonable estimate of its required future pension payments.

The auto manufacturers in this country found themselves in

a similar position in 2008; their unfunded pension liabilities were a major factor leading to the bankruptcy late in that year of two of the country's three major auto companies. Included in the bankruptcy negotiations was a restructuring of some of these liabilities.

Defined Contributions vs. Defined Benefit Retirement Funds

Defined Benefit Plan: The ultimate retirement payout is defined and guaranteed contractually.

In recent decades, employers have moved away from <u>defined (guaranteed) benefit</u> plans to <u>defined (guaranteed) contribution</u> plans. Under defined contribution plans, employers make regular contributions of a preset amount (generally a percentage of wages or salary earned) to an investment fund that is available to the employee upon retirement. Often, the employee is required to and/or is given the option to invest a percentage of his or her earnings in the same investment fund.

Defined Contribution Plan: The amount contributed is contractually set and invested in a retirement fund. The future retirement benefit depends on the returns earned by that fund.

A defined contribution plan, in contrast to a defined benefit plan, shifts the risk to the employee as to the amount of annual retirement income the plan will provide, since that depends upon how well the investment fund performs—that is, how much the investment earns over the years that the retirement fund is building. Moreover, the employee is often given some choice as to how "aggressive" he or she wishes to be (that is, how much risk he or she is willing to accept) in the investment of these retirement funds. The pros and cons of aggressive investing are the subject of the final chapter of this book.

Individual Retirement Accounts (IRAs)

Individual Retirement Account: Permits earners to invest pre-income-tax funds to build a retirement account.

The U.S. tax laws permit earners to invest a certain small percentage of their income in <u>individual retirement accounts</u> (<u>IRAs</u>); these funds are not subject to income tax when earned, but subsequent withdrawals (often years later) from the IRA (presumably following retirement) are taxed as ordinary income. Thus, the IRA offers two major tax advantages: (a) the tax is deferred and (b) the earnings on these "delayed" (not cancelled) tax payments are also tax-deferred. At a specified age (currently 70½) the owner of the IRA is required to withdraw and pay income tax on a specified minimum amount each year. The owner may, of course, withdraw larger amounts, all of which will be taxed as ordinary income.

Bear in mind that any postponement of a tax payment is desirable, since the cash that otherwise would have been used to pay the tax can be invested throughout the postponement periods, to the benefit of the taxpayer.

Annuities

At or near retirement, a person can purchase an <u>annuity</u> contract—typically from an insurance company—that will guarantee a certain monthly income. The purchase of the annuity contract may require installment payments (perhaps throughout the person's working life) or a lump-sum payment (perhaps at retirement). The price of the annuity will depend upon (a) the monthly payout amount that the buyer (i.e., future retiree) requires, and (b) the number of years during which the monthly amount will be paid. If the monthly payouts are to continue for life, then the life expectancy of the buyer is a key determinant of the cost of the annuity.

Finally, annuities come in two flavors: fixed and variable. In a fixed annuity, the monthly payout is set and does not vary with economic conditions or stock market performance. That is, the annuity provider (say, an insurance company) takes the risk that weak economic conditions or poor stock market performances may strain its ability to make the required annuity payments on schedule. In a <u>variable annuity</u>, the monthly payout varies, depending on economic conditions, and the <u>annuitant</u> accepts the inherent economic risk, which may turn out to be in his or her favor or disfavor.

> <u>Annuity:</u> A specified income payable at stated intervals for a fixed or contingent period, often for the recipient's life.

> <u>Fixed Annuity:</u> Payments do not vary with future economic conditions.

> <u>Variable Annuity:</u> Payments vary with future economic conditions.

> <u>Annuitant:</u> The recipient of annuity payments.

Deferred Income Contracts

Some well-paid individuals negotiate with their employers for a portion of their compensation to be "deferred"—that is, paid to them upon retirement rather than currently. The motivations for this requested deferral are generally two: (1) to build additional retirement income, and (2) defer the income tax on this deferred compensation until retirement when the recipient's "tax bracket" (see chapter 1) may be lower. These plans must include certain restrictive provisions, acceptable to the taxing authorities, in order to qualify for tax deferral.

Note that "defined contribution plans" are a form of deferred income contract.

Contractual Savings

One important contractual arrangement for savings involves enrolling in your employer's "defined-contribution" (as contrasted with "defined-benefit") retirement plan. These plans are typically labeled something like 401-K plans, referencing an IRS provision that grants favorable tax treatment. These plans have two very attractive features: First, the employer makes a "matching" contribution to the saver's plan; the match arrangements vary widely among plans, but typically the employee must contribute a specified minimum percentage of his or her salary each pay period to qualify for the match. Second, the funds "contributed" by the employee are excluded from the employee's current taxable income; they will be taxed when the employee withdraws the funds after retirement. As a result of these deferrals, pretax earnings compound over time without being taxed. It would be hard to find other savings plans that provide such handsome returns.

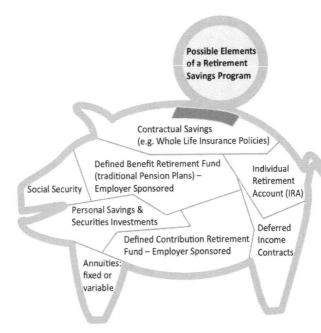

Possible Elements of a Retirement Savings Program

Contractual Savings (e.g. Whole Life Insurance Policies)

Defined Benefit Retirement Fund (traditional Pension Plans) – Employer Sponsored

Social Security

Individual Retirement Account (IRA)

Personal Savings & Securities Investments

Defined Contribution Retirement Fund – Employer Sponsored

Deferred Income Contracts

Annuities: fixed or variable

Nonetheless, too many employees pass up the opportunity to participate in these plans. Their primary reason is that they feel they cannot afford the reduction in their paychecks that the contractual "contributions" require. A second reason may be that these plans appear to be complex (although in truth they are fairly straightforward). A third reason may be simple procrastination or lethargy.

A so-called whole-life life insurance policy also commits the buyer to an ongoing stream of automatic savings. These are discussed later in this chapter.

One caveat before turning to insurance: politics (and particularly tax policy) have a good deal of influence on individual savings plans, particularly those related to financing one's retirement years. Remaining abreast of future changes—costs, risks, and opportunities—is essential for each of us.

Insurance

> *Insurance: Paying for catastrophe on the installment plan.*
> —*Anonymous*

Insurance policies can be purchased to protect against an almost infinite variety of risks. The iconic Lloyd's of London, for example, will insure athletic contests or parades against inclement weather, or professional pianists or athletes against arthritis or other disabling illnesses or events. Lloyd's got started by insuring cargo vessels at a time when these ships were still powered solely by wind!

We will consider here only insurance policies frequently purchased by individuals:

- medical insurance
- auto insurance
- homeowner's (or renter's) insurance
- general liability insurance
- long-term disability insurance
- life insurance (both term and whole life)

The price charged by the insurance company for the protection it provides to the buyer of the insurance policy (the insured) is called the <u>premium</u>. The <u>deductible</u> is the portion of the damage, injury, or loss claimed by the policy holder that must be paid by that policy holder before the insurance company's reimbursement commences. Consequently, a trade-off exists in most policies between the amount of the premium and the amount of the deductible. For example, if your driving record

Insurance Premium:
The price of the insurance protection for a specific period.

Deductible:
The portion of any insurance claim that must be paid by the policy holder.

Underwriting profits: Profit made by an insurance company because the amount paid out on claims is less than the amount it receives from the insurance premiums.

Float: Cash available for investment by insurance companies because of the time lag between the receipt of premiums and the subsequent payment of claims.

Group Medical Insurance: Medical insurance plans offered and subsidized by an employer.

Medicare: Federally provided medical insurance for senior citizens.

Medicaid: State-based medical insurance for low-income persons.

Medicare: Federally provided medical insurance for senior citizens.

Medicaid: State-based medical insurance for low-income persons.

suggests that you have fewer and less serious accidents than the average motorist, you should evaluate whether a higher deductible amount might result in a lower premium that would be cost effective for you.

It's worth bearing in mind that any insurance company has two primary sources of profits:

a. its underwriting profits
b. earnings on its float. Remember that all insurance protection is, of course, prepaid. Cash inflows from premiums occur before (sometimes years before) claims are paid out in cash. Meanwhile, this difference —the float—can be invested profitably for the benefit of the insurance company.

Medical Insurance

Unlike most other countries, the United States ties most medical insurance to employment; that is, the employer contracts for medical insurance for its employees and their dependents as a group and subsidizes to some extent the cost of that insurance. While medical insurance policies can be purchased directly by an individual (not through participation in his or her employer's plan), such policies typically are much more expensive than group medical insurance coverage obtained through an employer. This situation puts the self-employed individual or an employee of a small enterprise without a company medical plan at a significant economic disadvantage. Employed, single, healthy, young adults often feel that they can forego the company-sponsored medical plan and thereby avoid the employee portion of the premium. In general, foregoing all medical insurance coverage is an unwise decision, since illnesses and accidents are unpredictable.

In 2010, Congress passed legislation that mandates that all individuals carry medical insurance. As of mid-2012, it is unclear whether this legislation will survive challenges in Congress and if so, what effect it will have on medical insurance policies and the medical insurance industry. The federal government has for many years provided subsidized medical insurance for senior citizens (called Medicare) and the federal and state governments provide some medical coverage for those in poverty (generally called something like Medicaid).

Auto Insurance

Auto insurance comes in many pieces, one piece required and others optional to the auto owner. Auto insurance policies are written on autos, not on drivers (suggesting you be careful who you let drive your car!). Typically, state auto registration (to obtain car licenses) requires proof that the owner has insurance to pay for damages and injuries—collision and medical costs—inflicted by the auto on other cars and occupants of both cars; this is referred to as liability insurance. Individuals with substantial wealth (high net worth) will frequently carry extensive liability insurance—referred to as carrying high limits—for fear that the families of individuals severely injured or killed in an accident may file suit in an attempt to recover very extensive damages from the wealthy owner's auto causing the accident.

Unfortunately, one cannot be certain that all other cars carry liability insurance. Thus, auto owners typically carry another auto insurance piece—uninsured motorist coverage—to pay for collisions and injuries inflicted on them and their cars by other autos whose liability insurance is nonexistent or has lapsed.

The final piece is "comprehensive and collision insurance" to pay for repair of damages caused by accidents and so-called acts of God such as storms, floods, and tornados. These policies typically provide for a certain deductible amount, and obviously, policies with high deductibles have lower premiums than those with low deductibles. A high deductible would be the ideal choice if, in the event of an "act of God" or accident, paying the first $1,000 (or more) of costs would not be a financial hardship for you. Indeed, if the policy buyer concludes that the "total loss" of a car would not be a significant financial setback, he or she may elect to forego entirely a comprehensive and collision insurance coverage: referred to as self-insuring. For example, corporations operating a fleet of vehicles will self-insure the fleet for comprehensive and collision expenses. Why? To reduce their costs. They know from past experience what percentage of their vehicles will be involved in accidents and the average cost of repairs per accident. The corporation can budget on a statistical basis for these expenses.

However, it is exactly this wealthy individual or corporation that will opt for liability insurance with high limits to protect his or her (or the corporation's) net worth.

Limits: Insurance coverage up to high dollar amounts

Self-Insuring: Foregoing contracting for insurance from an outside supplier.

Homeowner's (Renter's) Insurance

Homeowner's insurance provides coverage for damage to or theft of a personal dwelling and its contents. It provides reimbursement for the repair or replacement of a home and its contents in the event of fire, windstorm, flood, landslide, a falling tree, or vandalism, as well as the replacement of furnishings that may be stolen.

Again, the insurance buyer can choose a low- or high-deductible amount depending upon how much risk he or she is willing to accept personally. The insurance company will adjust premiums to reflect its assessment of various conditions, such as the materials used in the construction of the house, its location, the probable replacement cost of the home furnishings, and the frequency of thefts and vandalisms in the community where the home is located. Typical premiums will be adjusted upward for homes located, for example, on steep slopes, in or near flood plains, in hurricane-prone areas of the country, and in high crime urban settings.

Note that rental properties and condominium properties are insured in part by policies purchased by the property owner, with the premiums included in the monthly rent or homeowner dues. The occupants, renters or condominium owners, typically insure the contents by means of a separate policy.

Individuals with extensive collections of valuable art or jewelry—attractive targets for thieves—will be required to <u>schedule</u> these valuables when they purchase insurance to cover these specific items.

<u>Scheduling:</u> Listing item by item for the insurance company all valuable art, jewelry, and other collections that are to be covered by the insurance policy.

Certain events, conditions, or items may be specifically excluded from coverage under standard insurance policies. For example, California homeowners' insurance policies generally exclude "earthquake coverage." Special earthquake insurance can be purchased but typically both the premiums and the deductibles are very high, and many owners elect not to insure against such an infrequent event. One can appreciate why an insurance company might be reluctant to write insurance on a large percentage of the homes near a particular earthquake fault, since any severe earthquake is likely to cause substantial damage to all the homes in the area, not to just one or a few. The more diversified—geographically and otherwise—an insurance company's "book of business" is, the lower the probability that a single event will have a devastating effect on its profitability.

General Liability Insurance

Some individuals elect to buy what is referred to as a "blanket" or "umbrella" liability policy. These days, juries seem to award increasingly large damages in lawsuits alleging carelessness, malfeasance, unsafe property conditions, reckless driving, less-than-adequate disclosure, failure to exercise good judgment or "duty of care," or simply acting imprudently—particularly if the defendant appears to have substantial net worth. The risks that may lead to these high awards are often not readily apparent. Some examples: the director of a corporation might be sued by shareholders for exercising poor judgment; the executor of a substantial estate may be sued by heirs or those who believe they are the proper heirs; the owner of a home swimming pool may be sued by parents of a drowned child for negligence in not preventing access to the pool. Should a legal judgment go against one of these persons, resulting in a very substantial monetary judgment, a large portion of a wealthy but uninsured person's net worth could be thereby consumed. Although such judgments are infrequent, they can be devastating. Because of their infrequency, the premiums on umbrella liability insurance policies with high limits are quite reasonable.

Umbrella Liability Policy: Provides liability protection over and above the protection provided by auto, homeowner and other underlying insurance policies.

An added advantage of most liability policies is that the insurance company will assist in the legal defense of the insured person. Successful defense is, of course, beneficial to both the insured and the insurance company. Defenses are often lengthy and very expensive.

Overinsuring or Underinsuring

Some individuals overinsure—that is, they carry insurance that provides reimbursement for minor losses. They want to avoid virtually all insurable losses or costs, including doctor and prescription drug expenses, and even minor auto damage. Insurance companies are delighted to write such insurance, but be aware that the premiums will be high for these policies.

More reasonably, individuals should insure against catastrophic (or at least semicatastrophic) events. Most people would consider a fire that completely gutted their home to be a catastrophic event, well worth insuring against. Similarly, an illness

Write: To sell an insurance policy

21

that required lengthy hospitalization and sophisticated medical testing and treatment would be catastrophic; carrying major medical insurance (and disability insurance as well) is wise. On the other hand, carrying auto damage insurance with only $100 deductible (that is, the owner pays the first $100 of repair costs; the insurance company pays the balance) is very expensive and perhaps unwise. Similarly, one can select medical insurance with various deductible amounts (typically an annual deductible); the individual can select the trade-off between deductible amount and insurance premium that is optimal for his or her family's financial circumstance.

Long-Term Disability Insurance

AD&D Insurance: Provides payment in the event of death by accident (not disease) or loss of a limb.

Long-term disability insurance policies provide for periodic (typically monthly) payments to the insured if he or she becomes disabled and can no longer work. Many employer-provided group insurance packages include long-term disability insurance, as well as group medical insurance, but these can also be purchased individually. For a relatively young worker with substantial family obligations, this form of insurance may be at least as important (if not more) as life insurance. Indeed, another component of many employer-provided group insurance plans is so-called AD&D insurance—accidental death and dismemberment insurance.

Life Insurance

Life Insurance: Provides a stated payment in the event of death during the term of the policy.

Term Life Insurance: Lapses at the end of the term, typically one year.

The variety among life insurance policies is wide, but the two basic flavors are "term" and "whole life."

Term insurance is generally written for one year at a time. If during that year, the insured dies, his or her beneficiary (typically, family) receives the lump-sum stipulated in the policy. If death does not occur, the policy terminates at the end of the year with no residual benefits to the insured—but, of course, the insured may decide to renew the policy for the following year.

Employer group insurance plans often include a certain (minimal) amount of term life insurance, perhaps enough to cover what are called "final expenses." But many plans also permit the employee to increase the amount of the insurance at his or her own expense, and often at quite attractive premium rates.

Importantly, insurance companies will not agree to sell a term life insurance policy to an individual who is at death's door – that is, someone who has a terminal illness. In insurance parlance, the life insurance company reserves the right to refuse to insure (or renew the term life insurance policy of) a person who has unacceptable preexisting medical conditions, such as terminal cancer, Parkinson's disease, and HIV/AIDS.

Some term insurance policies, however, include a provision that guarantees the insured person of continued insurability for a certain period of time. Of course, the insurance company will charge a higher premium for a policy that has this added guaranteed insurability provision.

Guaranteed Insurability: An add-on provision to some term life policies that guarantees that the life insurance may be renewed at the end of the current term.

So-called whole-life insurance policies are really two financial vehicles combined into a single contract: insurance for loss of life, and a savings plan. They are considerably more expensive than term policies. In addition to the death benefit and the guaranteed insurability inherent in whole-life insurance contracts, these policies provide for the buildup over the years of a "cash value"—an amount that is available to the insured if and when the insured cancels the contract. Also, the insured may be able to borrow this "cash value" to meet emergency needs.

Whole-Life Insurance Policies: Combined in one contract: insurance for loss of life and a plan for accumulating savings.

Life insurance policies providing high death benefits will typically require the insurance purchaser to undergo a medical exam to assure that he or she has no disqualifying preexisting medical conditions.

So should individuals buy "term" or "whole life" policies? Younger persons with substantial family responsibilities and limited current income should consider term policies in order to maximize the "death benefit" obtainable for the amount that he or she can afford to spend on life insurance. Even those with moderate family responsibilities may decide to invest separately in "life insurance" and "savings" by buying lower-cost term insurance and using other invest vehicles to accumulate savings. Still, others may feel that the contractual or forced savings that is inherent in the whole-life policy enforces a good "savings discipline."

Conclusion

Remember: insurance just shifts to the insurance company the economic costs associated with certain risks; it does not eliminate the risks.

Estate Planning

Much of the discussion in this chapter relates indirectly to the subject of underlineestate planning. The emphasis earlier in this chapter has been preparing for retirement: assuring oneself of sufficient funds to continue a reasonable lifestyle between retirement and death, which will occur in an uncertain number of years after retirement. So, gruesome as it may sound, planning for death, as well as for retirement, is essential.

People have various plans for postretirement and postdeath. Some seek to **bequeath** at their death more than a token amount to their children and/or grandchildren. Others have philanthropic plans (plans to be generous to charities) that they wish to fulfill later in their lives or at death.

Estate planning can be simple or complex. At the very least, every adult—single, married, divorced, with children, childless, wealthy or poor—should have a **will**. Wills, like estate plans, can be simple or complex. At the least, they should name an executor: a person who will wind up the deceased person's affairs, pay outstanding bills including current taxes, and distribute both physical and monetary assets according to the wishes of the deceased, as spelled out in his or her will. And the will certainly should designate guardians for surviving minor children.

Many a family squabble has been avoided by a carefully drawn, comprehensive, but not necessarily elaborate, will. But disappointingly, a very large percentage of adults in this country do not have a will, often feeling that the size of their estate precludes the need.

As persons mature, gaining both wealth and altered family conditions, estate plans get more complex, with the complexity often driven by efforts to minimize estate taxes. Estate tax rates and allowed deductions have varied widely in recent years.

Meanwhile, accountants and lawyers have devised ingenious and complicated ways to reduce or postpone an estate's future death tax obligations. Some of these make good sense, but not all. Typically, the more complex the estate plan (some involving complex trusts and other legal constructs),

a. the greater the loss of flexibility to change plans as

family situations (births, marriages, divorces, deaths) or financial conditions change (large financial gains or losses); and

b.   the greater the legal and administrative costs associated with both conceptualizing and drafting the plan in legal terms and, later, executing it.

Personally, I think that (1) flexibility is often underrated as an objective of estate planning, and (2) paying a modest amount of estate taxes is a wealthy citizen's reasonable obligation.

A final thought: many people postpone making sizeable gifts to either charities or living individuals (including family members) until death (gifts by bequest). Indeed, the concern that one might "run out of money before death" is a good reason for postponing gift making. For those with generously adequate means, giving while alive has much to recommend it. Most importantly, helping others is very satisfying. But gifts during one's lifetime can also be very tax efficient; the law permits gift-tax free giving to individuals subject to two limitations: a maximum annual amount per recipient, and a maximum lifetime amount for the donor. These limits apply to gifts to individuals, not to charitable gifts. A more thorough discussion of giving is beyond the scope of this book.

Review Questions for Chapter 2:

1.   Why might one choose a savings account (time deposit) for emergency savings rather than a certificate of deposit (CD)?
2.   Why do more and more companies use "defined contribution" rather than "defined benefit" pension plans for their employees?
3.   What does it mean to "overinsure"? What are the costs and risks of overinsuring?
4.   Why might an individual choose to self-insure certain risks?
5.   What provisions should be included in a person's will when he or she is twenty years old? Thirty years old? Forty years old? Seventy years old?

Chapter Three

COMPOUND INTEREST AND LEVERAGE

Compound interest is the eighth wonder of the world. He who understands it earns it . . . he who doesn't, pays it.

—Albert Einstein

The title of this chapter, like the last, appears to link two disparate subjects. They appear together here for two reasons: they both are (a) powerful financial tools, and (b) fundamental to improving your financial well-being.

Given Einstein's wisdom, let's consider <u>compound interest</u> first, and contrast it with <u>simple interest</u>.

Compound Interest

Suppose you put $1,000 into a savings account that promises a 6 percent return for ten years. Does this mean that at the end of ten years your account will be worth $1,060—your original $1,000 plus 6 percent? No, the promised return is annual, and furthermore, it is based each year on the increasing balance in the account. This compounding of the interest is key. At the end of year one, your balance will have increased by 6 percent: from $1,000 to $1,060. The following year, your balance will increase by 6 percent again, only this time it is 6 percent of the $1,060 that you had in your account at the beginning of year two. Six percent of $1,070 is $63, and so your balance at the end of year two is $1,123. In year three, you get 6 percent of that $1,123 added to your account, $67, resulting in a year-three balance of $1,191.

<u>Compound Interest:</u> Interest for the period is added to the principal balance. In each subsequent period the interest is calculated on the increasing principal balance.

<u>Simple Interest:</u> The interest for each period is calculated on the original principal balance, without regard to any previous interest payments.

This process continues as shown in the table below so that every year a larger interest amount is added to your account.

At the end of ten years—assuming you withdraw nothing throughout the ten years—the value of your account will be about $1,791.

If the interest were *not* compounding, you would receive 6 percent of $1,000 ($60) each year for ten years. That would add up $600 of interest earnings and a final balance of $1,600—as compared to the $1,791 balance that you earned with compounding interest. That's almost 15 percent more because of compounding!

Compound vs. Simple Interest

| | Account Balance | |
Year	Simple Interest	Compound Interest
0	$1,000	$1,000
1	$1,060	$1,060
2	$1,120	$1,124
3	$1,180	$1,191
4	$1,240	$1,262
5	$1,300	$1,338
6	$1,360	$1,419
7	$1,420	$1,504
8	$1,480	$1,594
9	$1,540	$1,689
10	$1,600	$1,791

Present Value Factors

Return on investment (ROI): sometimes referred to as the internal rate of return (IRR). The earnings interest rate inherent in an investment (outflow of cash), followed by a series of returns (cash inflows).

Appendix A to this chapter sets forth the factors necessary to calculate the effects of compounding interest at various interest rates for various numbers of years. Two sets of tables are included, the first assuming a single payment and the second annual payments.

The following examples illustrate the use of these factors; the examples are labeled:

    a.   calculate present values;

b. calculate future values; and
c. calculate (by trial and error) the effective interest rate (<u>ROI</u>).

Single Payment Present Value Factors (SPPVF)
(See table 1 in appendix A for the factors.)

a. In five years, David is scheduled to receive $5,000 from a friend. He needs the money now, and plans to negotiate with his friend for early payment. He believes that the interest rate relevant to both his friend and himself is 10 percent. In this example, we know the future value, the interest rate, and the number of years; we seek the present value, V.

V = 5,000 × (SPPVF, 10%, five years)
V = 5,000 × 0.6209 = $3,104.50

b. Judy plans to buy a $10,000 three-year CD offering a 3 percent interest rate. How much will she have in this account at the end of the three years? In this example, we know the present value ($10,000), the number of years, and the interest rate, and we seek the future value, F.

$10,000 = F × (SPPVF, 3%, three years)
$10,000 = F × 0.9151
F = $10,000 ÷ 0.9151 = $10,927.77

c. Carol is promised by her wealthy uncle a bequest of $250,000 at the time of his death. The uncle has a remaining life expectancy of fifteen years. Because Carol is eager to purchase a home, her uncle has offered to give her $125,000 now rather than the bequest. What is the effective interest rate inherent in this "trade"? In this example, we know the present value, the future value, and the number of years. We seek the interest rate (i); we can find it by trial and error:

Try 7%:
$125,000 = $250,000 × (SPPVF, 7%, fifteen years)
$250,000 × (0.5083) = $127,075

Since $125,000 and $127,075 are very close, the inherent interest rate is just slightly higher than 7 percent.

Annual Payments Present Value Factors (APPFV)
(See table 2 in appendix A for the factors.)

a. Mark is owed by Adam, his brother, a $2,500 payment each year for the next eight years. Mark has an opportunity to make a major investment earning a handsome return, and seeks an accelerated payment from his brother. He believes that the present worth of these promised future payments, calculated at 10 percent, would be fair to both his brother and him. In this example, we know the annual payment amount, the number of years, and the interest rate. We seek the present value, V.

$$V = 2,500 \times (\text{APPVF, 10 percent, eight years})$$
$$= 2,500 \times 5.747 = \$14,367.50$$

b. Caroline has a "nest egg" of $750,000 upon retirement. She plans to invest this sum to earn 7 percent. Her current remaining life expectancy is twenty years. How much can Caroline withdraw each year for twenty years and have nothing left at the end of twenty years? In this example, we know the present value, the number of years, and the interest rate. We seek the annual payment (withdrawal), W.

$$\$750,000 = W \times (\text{APPVF, 7\%, twenty years})$$
$$= W \times 10.594$$
$$W = \$70,795$$

c. Fred is considering a $250,000 investment that is expected to provide a $40,000 per year return for thirty years. What is the expected return on this investment? In this example, we know the present value, the annual return (payment), and the number of years. We now solve, by trial and error, for the interest rate, i.

$$\$250,000 = \$40,000 \times (\text{APPVF, i\%, twenty years})$$
$$\text{Try 20\%} - \$40,000 \times 4.870 = \$194,800$$

Therefore, the ROI is less than 20%,

$$\text{Try 15\%} - \$40,000 \times 6.259 = \$250,360$$

Therefore, this investment offers a 15% ROI.

Appendix B contains five more examples regarding compound interest and present value factors worth careful study.

Debt Leverage: For Individuals

Many people pick up the idea early in their lives that "being in debt" should be avoided, that it is rather unseemly to owe money. Although most cannot avoid borrowing in order to buy a home, many seek to pay off all their debt as soon as possible.

Let me suggest that borrowing—that is, debt—is neither bad nor good. <u>Debt leverages</u> our financial positions. Sometimes the leverage is positive, improving our overall financial position, and sometimes leverage is negative.

Take a simple example: you can borrow at an annual interest rate of 5 percent and use the money to make a risk-free investment earning 8 percent per year. Moreover, you can sell your investment and pay off your borrowing at any time with no penalty. That set of transactions is a "no-brainer." If those assumptions are attainable (they are not in the real world!), you have leveraged your financial position positively.

Example 1:

Now suppose Carson is considering a mining project that requires him to invest $500,000 at the outset. The annual <u>cash flow</u> return to him as an investor is expected to be $150,000 per year for six years and the project has no <u>salvage value</u> at the end of six years when the mine is expected to be exhausted. Following the procedures illustrated in the previous few pages and in the Appendices to this chapter, he calculates the ROI on this project to be approximately 20 percent, as follows:

$$V = \$150,000 \times (\text{APPVF, six years, 20 \%})$$
$$V = \$150,000 \times 3.326$$
$$V = \$498,900, \text{ very near the } \$500,000 \text{ investment.}$$

Carson considers this 20 percent return on investment to be attractive, given the risks inherent in such mining projects.

Carson now considers the question of whether he should borrow a portion of the $500,000 to be invested. He believes that debt leverage might improve his return. Carson's bank has offered to lend him $200,000 for six years at 7.5 percent interest, with repayment of the principal at the end of the six years.

To analyze this leverage opportunity, consider the cash flows: inflows and outflows of the project (mining) combined with those of the financing. The cash flows for this project (in thousands of dollars) are:

Debt Leverage: results from an individual or a corporation borrowing funds to make investments. The resulting leverage improves (positive leverage) or worsens (negative leverage) the financial results for the individual or company.

Cash Flow: the value of cash paid out (outflow) and received (inflow).

Salvage Value: the monetary amount that can be realized by disposing of an investment at the end of its useful life.

	Year						
	0	**1**	**2**	**3**	**4**	**5**	**6**
Invest	-500						
Borrow	+200						
Pay Interest		-15	-15	-15	-15	-15	-15
Cash Inflow		+150	+150	+150	+150	+150	+150
Repay Debt							-200
Net	-300	+135	+135	+135	+135	+135	-65
Total: +310							

The net initial investment is $300,000: ($500,000 less $200,000). The mining project's annual cash inflow of $150,000 is unaffected by the financing. Carson must pay $15,000 of interest annually and repay the borrowed amount, $200,000, at the end of year six.

Year	Cash Flow	SPPVF at 30%	Annual Present Worth
0	-300	1.0	-300
1	+135	0.7692	+104
2	+135	0.5917	+80
3	+135	0.4552	+61
4	+135	0.3501	+47
5	+135	0.2693	+36
6	-65	0.2072	-13
		Total:	+ 15

The ROI inherent in the $300,000 net initial investment is slightly above 30 percent, much higher than when Carson uses no debt financing. He is potentially realizing positive debt leverage.

But before getting too excited about this revised return, Carson should note that he is still "at risk" for the full $500,000; that is, he must repay the bank whether or not the mining project proves out. Thus, he has increased—leveraged up—his return but not diminished his personal risk, even though he is investing at the outset only $300,000, not $500,000.

Now suppose this mining venture does not live up to expectations and the annual return is $100,000, only two-thirds of the original estimate. Carson's cash outflows associated with the borrowing are unchanged. Now the return on the $300,000 investment is less than 5 percent, well lower than the return figured without bank financing. The debt has leveraged the project negatively.

Example 2:

A danger for any individual is that he or she may easily walk blindly into a situation that unwittingly delivers negative leverage. Suppose Ms. McCarthy is committed to making monthly payments into the 401-K plan operated by her employer. She has invested in a mix of stocks and bonds that her investment advisor suggests should, over the long term, deliver about an 8 percent annual return. Ms. McCarthy now decides to redecorate the living room of her home; the cost of this project exceeds the amount she had set aside for it, and she uses her credit card to cover the extra costs. Ms. McCarthy then finds that it will take her about a year to pay off the credit card balance that she has run up. Unpaid balances on her credit card accrue interest at a rate of 18 percent. Thus, Ms. McCarthy is now involved in negative leverage—paying 18 percent or more in credit card interest, while earning 8 percent on her 401-K.

Suffering this negative leverage may be wise for Ms. McCarthy for a short period of time rather than interrupting her regular contributions to her 401-K. However, I am amazed at the number of people who routinely run outstanding balances on their credit cards while having funds invested in the securities markets. When I ask them if they really anticipate they can earn more than 18 or 19 percent in the securities market, they sheepishly respond, "Gee, I guess not."

We need to remember that money is <u>fungible</u>—an economist's term that means it can be used for alternative purposes. Money doesn't come with labels like, "This is for investing in common stock," or "This is for debt repayment." In an effort to be disciplined in pursuing sound financing policies—a worthy objective—some people become blind to the benefits of monetary fungibility. It would be perfectly reasonable for Ms. McCarthy to <u>liquidate</u> some investments to repay "expensive" debt. But then she needs to be disciplined about getting back on her long-term financial plan.

Fungible: Fungible money is not restricted as to use, and therefore can be used for various alternative purposes.

Liquidate: Sell, realize value from

And bear in mind that compound interest also applies to outstanding borrowing, as illustrated in one of the examples in appendix B (the postponement of repayments on a student loan). Borrowing on credit cards is mighty costly borrowing. An individual who "maxes" out his borrowing on two or three credit cards quickly gets himself in an untenable debt position: the compounding of the interest on this debt outstrips the rate at which he can make monthly payments on his credit cards from his earnings. The result is an ever-growing debt load that may well lead to personal bankruptcy.

So Einstein might have expanded his definition of compound interest to include "danger" as well as "wonder" of the world.

Appendix A

Table 1

Single Payment Present Value Factors

	Interest Rates													
Year	3%	4%	5%	6%	7%	8%	9%	10%	12%	15%	18%	20%	25%	30%
1	0.9709	0.9615	0.9524	0.9434	0.9346	0.9259	0.9174	0.9091	0.8929	0.8696	0.8475	0.8333	0.8	0.7692
2	0.9426	0.9246	0.9070	0.8900	0.8734	0.8573	0.8417	0.8264	0.7972	0.7561	0.7182	0.6944	0.64	0.5917
3	0.9151	0.8890	0.8138	0.8396	0.8163	0.7938	0.7722	0.7513	0.7118	0.6575	0.6086	0.5787	0.572	0.4552
4	0.8885	0.8548	0.8227	0.7921	0.7629	0.7350	0.7084	0.6830	0.6355	0.5718	0.5158	0.4823	0.4096	0.3501
5	0.8626	0.8219	0.7835	0.7473	0.7130	0.6806	0.6499	0.6209	0.5674	0.4972	0.4371	0.4019	0.3277	0.2693
6	0.8375	0.7903	0.7462	0.7050	0.6663	0.6302	0.5963	0.5645	0.5066	0.4323	0.3704	0.3349	0.2621	0.2072
7	0.8131	0.7599	0.7107	0.6651	0.6227	0.5835	0.5470	0.5132	0.4523	0.3759	0.3139	0.2791	0.2097	0.1594
8	0.7894	0.7307	0.6768	0.6274	0.5820	0.5403	0.5019	0.4665	0.4039	0.3269	0.266	0.2326	0.1678	0.1226
9	0.7664	0.7026	0.6446	0.5919	0.5439	0.5002	0.4604	0.4241	0.3606	0.2843	0.2255	0.1938	0.1342	0.0943
10	0.7441	0.6756	0.6139	0.5584	0.5083	0.4632	0.4224	0.3855	0.3220	0.2472	0.1911	0.1615	0.1074	0.0725
12	0.7014	0.6246	0.5568	0.4970	0.4440	0.3971	0.3555	0.3186	0.2567	0.1869	0.1372	0.1122	0.0687	0.0429
15	0.6419	0.5553	0.4810	0.4173	0.3624	0.3152	0.2745	0.2394	0.1827	0.1229	0.0835	0.0649	0.0352	0.0195
18	0.5874	0.4936	0.4155	0.3503	0.2959	0.2502	0.2120	0.1799	0.1300	0.0808	0.0508	0.0376	0.018	0.0089
20	0.5537	0.4560	0.3769	0.3118	0.2584	0.2145	0.1784	0.1486	0.1037	0.0611	0.0365	0.0261	0.0115	0.0053
25	0.4776	0.3751	0.2953	0.2330	0.1842	0.1460	0.1160	0.0923	0.0588	0.0304	0.016	0.0105	0.0038	0.0014
30	0.4120	0.3083	0.2314	0.1741	0.1314	0.0994	0.0753	0.0573	0.0334	0.0151	0.007	0.0042	0.0012	0.0004
40	0.3066	0.2083	0.1420	0.0972	0.0668	0.0460	0.0318	0.0221	0.0107	0.0037	0.0013	0.0007	0.0001	0
50	0.2281	0.1407	0.0872	0.0543	0.0339	0.0213	0.0134	0.0085	0.0035	0.0009	0.0003	0.0001	0	0

Table 2

Annual Payment Present Value Factors

	Interest Rates													
Year	3%	4%	5%	6%	7%	8%	9%	10%	12%	15%	18%	20%	25%	30%
1	0.9709	0.9615	0.9524	0.9434	0.9346	0.9259	0.9174	0.9091	0.8929	0.8696	0.9709	0.9615	0.9524	0.9434
2	1.9135	1.8861	1.8594	1.8334	1.8080	1.7833	1.7591	1.7355	1.6901	1.6257	1.9135	1.8861	1.8594	1.8334
3	2.8286	2.7751	2.7232	2.6730	2.6243	2.5771	2.5313	2.4869	2.4018	2.2832	2.8286	2.7751	2.7232	2.6730
4	3.7171	3.6299	3.5460	3.4651	3.3872	3.3121	3.2397	3.1699	3.0373	2.8550	3.7171	3.6299	3.5460	3.4651
5	4.5797	4.4518	4.3295	4.2124	4.1002	3.9927	3.8897	3.7908	3.6048	3.3522	4.5797	4.4518	4.3295	4.2124
6	5.4172	5.2421	5.0757	4.9173	4.7665	4.6229	4.4859	4.3553	4.1114	3.7845	5.4172	5.2421	5.0757	4.9173
7	6.2303	6.0021	5.7864	5.5824	5.3893	5.2064	5.0330	4.8684	4.5638	4.1604	6.2303	6.0021	5.7864	5.5824
8	7.0197	6.7327	6.4632	6.2098	5.9713	5.7466	5.5348	5.3349	4.9676	4.4873	7.0197	6.7327	6.4632	6.2098
9	7.7861	7.4353	7.1078	6.8017	6.5152	6.2469	5.9952	5.7590	5.3282	4.7716	7.7861	7.4353	7.1078	6.8017
10	8.5302	8.1109	7.7217	7.3601	7.0236	6.7101	6.4177	6.1446	5.6502	5.0188	8.5302	8.1109	7.7217	7.3601
12	9.9540	9.3851	8.8633	8.3838	7.9427	7.5361	7.1607	6.8137	6.1944	5.4206	9.9540	9.3851	8.8633	8.3838
15	11.938	11.118	10.380	9.712	9.108	8.559	8.061	7.606	6.811	5.847	11.938	11.118	10.380	9.712
18	13.754	12.659	11.690	10.828	10.059	9.372	8.756	8.201	7.250	6.128	13.754	12.659	11.690	10.828
20	14.877	13.590	12.462	11.470	10.594	9.818	9.129	8.514	7.469	6.259	14.877	13.590	12.462	11.470
25	17.413	15.622	14.094	12.783	11.654	10.675	9.823	9.077	7.843	6.464	17.413	15.622	14.094	12.783
30	19.600	17.292	15.372	13.765	12.409	11.258	10.274	9.427	8.055	6.566	19.600	17.292	15.372	13.765
40	23.115	19.793	17.159	15.046	13.332	11.925	10.757	9.779	8.244	6.642	23.115	19.793	17.159	15.046
50	25.730	21.482	18.256	15.762	13.801	12.233	10.962	9.915	8.304	6.661	25.730	21.482	18.256	15.762

Appendix B

Additional Examples

Example 1:

Molly is a twenty-five-year-old college graduate with three years of work experience who decides that she should start saving for retirement. Given her modest salary, she decides that she can afford to invest only $5,000 per year, but she has thirty working years before she plans to retire early at age fifty-five. She plans to make this same investment in each of those thirty years and withdraw nothing until retirement. Looking over the long history of the United States stock market, she decides that, even with the inevitable ups and downs in annual performance, a 7 percent average annual return over thirty years is conservative.

Using the second table in appendix A: (APPVF), 7 %, thirty years from appendix A,

We start by determining the present value of the $5,000 payments:

$$= 12.409 \times \$5,000 = \$62,045$$

But we need to determine its future value, that is, after thirty years.

Using the SPPVF table:
$$62,045 = V \times 0.1314.$$
$$V = \$472,184$$

Note that her value at retirement is 2.6 times the $150,000 ($5,000 per year for thirty years) she invested over her thirty-year working career.

Alternatively, suppose Molly decides that in order to enjoy her youth and accrue a few salary increases, she will postpone investing for retirement for ten years, until she is thirty-five years old. But she thinks she will need the full $472,184 calculated in the previous paragraph to support an early, long and comfortable retirement. How much will she need to invest per year for the last twenty years of her working life (age thirty-five to fifty-five) in order to accumulate that amount assuming average stock market returns of 7 percent per year? If she is saving for fewer years, but wants the same ending amount, she has to invest:

$$V = [\$472,184 \times 0.2524] \div 10.594$$
$$V = \$11,250$$

Why so much? Because in this second scenario, Molly is giving up the benefit of the money she would gain from compounding interest for those first ten years, and she is reducing from thirty to twenty the number of years of savings.

Example 2:

Chris, another young college graduate, has an outstanding balance on his student loans of $43,000; the loans have interest rates of 5 percent. Because he is starting a new music business into which he needs to make a sizeable personal investment, he elects to postpone for ten years the installment payments that serve to reduce this outstanding balance. However, the 5 percent interest compounds during the postponement period. In order to find out how much he will owe in ten years, Chris asks himself: at a 5 percent interest rate, what will the outstanding loan be at the end of the ten-year postponement, given that it now has a present value of $43,000? To perform this calculation, use the SPPVF. The algebraic calculation is

$43,000 = V \times 0.6319$
$V = $69,049$

The loan balance increases by about 60 percent.

Example 3:

Sam is tempted to buy a large piece of vacant property in a highly desirable location where twenty years from now he will build his dream house. He has watched prices of homes and homesites escalate in recent years, and Sam believes that he would have to pay three times as much for this piece of property in twenty years. Is a three-time return over twenty years (ignoring property taxes and any other upkeep costs) a good investment? In order to answer that question, Sam asks himself, *at what interest rate is $3 received in twenty years equivalent to $1 today*? Sam uses the same formula that Chris has used in the previous example but with a different unknown. He assumes the future value (3) and knows the present value (1) and seeks the present value factor that will satisfy the equation:

$1 = (SPPVF for twenty years) \times 3

The first table in appendix A provides the needed factors, at twenty years:

At i equals 5%: $3 \times (0.3769) = 1.13
At i equals 7%: $3 \times (0.2524) = 0.76

Therefore, by interpolation, the interest rate (i.e., the annualized return on investment) is about 5.5 percent, hardly a bonanza. Could Sam find an alternative investment (perhaps one with less inherent risk than the homesite) where he could invest his money for twenty years at a rate greater than or equal to 5.5 percent per year, and then use those funds to buy his dream site?

A bit more complicated calculation aids the decision whether to rent or buy a home or to lease or purchase a car. The complications arise from the fact that the analyst is challenged to forecast cash flows—rent, home purchase and resale values, and home upkeep costs—for many years into the future.

Example 4:

Gretchen is an executive at Roller Skates Inc. and is evaluating two proposals for a solar system for the company's factory building. Each should provide the company with net savings of $100,000 per year. Alternative A costs $300,000 and has an expected life of five years, while alternative B has a cost of $400,000 and has an expected life of ten years. In summary,

Alternative A has a <u>payback</u> of three years, while B's payback is four years; however, A and B have different useful lives. For Gretchen to evaluate A and B fairly, she needs to know the return-on-investment (ROI) for each—that is, what are her returns on the $300,000 and $400,000 investment in A and B provided by an annual $100,000 savings for five (and ten) years? To evaluate this question, Gretchen uses the second table in appendix A (annual payments.) As in Sam's case, she seeks to find the interest rate (ROI) that satisfies the equations, as follows:

Payback: the original investment divided by the annual return from the investment in years.

> Try 20% rate –
>
> $V = \$100,000 \times (2.991)$
> $= \$299,100$, or almost exactly the $300,000 invested. Therefore, the return on investment is just slightly less than 20 percent.

For Alternative B with a ten-year life, the present value of the annual savings, again at 20 percent, is $100,000 \times (4.192) = \$419,200$. Therefore the ROI is slightly greater than 20 percent.

By the way, the returns on Alternatives A and B are so similar that Gretchen may well decide that other factors, such as technological improvements over the next few years, argue for accepting Alternative A.

Example 5:

Sarah has read the magazine Monster Truck Frenzy consistently for twenty years and expects to continue to read it faithfully for many more years. The magazine offers her several options for a six-year renewal of her subscription. She may make a one-time payment now of $178 or a payment of $45 now and that amount again at the beginning of each of the next five years. Which is the better deal for her? In effect, she may make an extra $133 payment ($178 minus $45) now to avoid making five $45 payments at the end of each of years one, two, three, four, and on the face of it, the lump-sum payment looks quite attractive—and it is; her $133 payment provides her five years of $45 annual savings, an annualized return of over 25 percent:

At 25%: $45 x (3.277) = $147, or somewhat more than her $133 extra investment now. So the return of investment is somewhat more than 25 percent.

Of course, Sarah is also accepting the risk that a change in ownership or editorial policy of Monster Truck Frenzy during these six years will cause her to lose interest in the magazine long before the six years are up!

Review Questions for Chapter 3:

[Single Payment]

1. A $150 payment that will be received in ten years has what present value when discounted at 7 percent?
2. The same $150 payment received in the same ten years has what present value when discounted at 15 percent?
3. $2,500 invested at a 10 percent rate of return for fifteen years will have what future value?
4. The same $2,500 invested at a 15 percent rate for the same fifteen years will have what future value?

[Annual Payment]

5. Payments of $400 to be received at the end of each year for fifteen years have what present value when discounted at 10 percent?
6. Payments of the same $400 for the same fifteen years have what present value when discounted at 15 percent?
7. If a person invests $100,000 now at a rate of return of 10 percent, how much can that person withdraw each year for twenty years, depleting the investment to zero at the end of year twenty?
8. If the person invests the same $100,000 but at a rate of 5 percent, how much can be withdrawn each year for twenty years?

[Combined Use of Factors]

9. Consider an investment of $325,000 in a boat to be rented/chartered for ten years, then sold for an estimated $100,000. There is an annual charter fee income of $125,000. What interest rate, i, will this investment earn?

Answers to Review Problems

1. $150 × 0.5083 = $76.25
2. $150 × 0.2472 = $37.08
3. $2,500 ÷ 0.2394 = $10,443
4. $2,500 ÷ 0.1229 = $20,341
5. $400 × 7.606 = $3,042
6. $400 × 5.847 = $2,339
7. $100,000 ÷ 8.514 = $ 11,745
8. $100,000 ÷ 12.462 = $8,024
9. $325,000 = [$125,000 × (APPVF, ten years, interest rate i) + ($100,000)] × (SPPVF, ten years, interest rate i)
    Try i = 10 percent: Present value of future cash incomes = $335,000. Thus, ROI is just a bit more than 10 percent.

Chapter Four

SOURCES OF CREDIT FOR INDIVIDUALS

Wealth: Owing nothing.

—Hungarian Proverb

Money is the poor people's credit card.

—Marshall McLuhan

Previous chapters introduced the subject of lending by banks and credit card issuers—major sources of credit for individuals. This chapter expands that discussion to consider other sources. Borrowing by corporations is covered in chapter 5. Credit markets, relevant to individual investing, as well as to corporate borrowing, are discussed in chapter 6.

Loans among Individuals

Lending and borrowing among friends or family members is surely not an "organized" market. But at the outset of this discussion, we should remind ourselves that these person-to-person credit transactions aggregate to a very large amount. However, we cannot usefully generalize about these transactions, since their terms vary hugely dependent upon the relationship between borrower and lender. For example, loans among congenial family members may be on very favorable terms to the borrower. Nevertheless, all person-to-person borrowing—regardless of who the parties are—should be well documented with formal agreements executed. From many reports, we know that some intrafamily borrowing, particularly if not well documented, can lead to bitterness and estrangement.

High-Cost Personal Borrowing

Even individuals who you might think could not borrow, because their incomes are low or nonexistent or because they are already overburdened with debt, may still be able to borrow additional funds, but only at very high interest rates.

Payday Loans: Very short-term loans at high interest rates, typically to be repaid from the borrower's next paycheck.

One sees storefronts scattered around most cities advertising payday loans. These loans may charge, for example, a $10 fee on an "advance" of $210 to be repaid from the next salary check, due in ten days. The borrower receives $200 and promises to repay $210 in 10 days (note that the $10 retained by the lender is just 5 percent of the net amount borrowed—$200). That may not sound so bad, as we are accustomed to evaluating annualized interest charges. But wait a minute, 5 percent for just a ten-day loan is quite another matter. If you were to use this source of borrowing on a regular basis, you would be paying that $10 fee many times. There are 36.5 ten-day periods in a year (365 days divided by ten days); therefore an approximation of the annual interest charge on this payday loan is 36.5 ten-day periods times 5 percent per period, or 182.5 percent per year—a very, very high interest charge indeed. Thus, these "storefront" or "payday loans" should be viewed as last-ditch sources of small amounts for very short periods. Avoid them if at all possible.

Lay-Away Plans: Permit shoppers, for a fee, to reserve purchases, paying for the purchases in several monthly installments, and receiving the merchandise only when the full price has been paid.

Here is another innocuous-sounding, but very expensive, opportunity for the struggling retail shopper to borrow a little money. Many of the largest retailers in this country offer lay-away plans, permitting the early holiday shopper to select holiday gifts valued at, say, $100, place them "on hold" with a $10 (10 percent) down payment plus a small fee of about $5. The shopper makes two more payments during the next two months running up to the holidays. That $5 fee (which is in effect interest) on $90 of borrowing for only two months amounts to an annualized interest rate of about 44 percent. While the $5 fee sounds trivial in amount, the benefits received by the consumer are even more trivial! Moreover, the retailer is taking no risk; if the shopper doesn't complete the lay-away payments, he or she will not receive the merchandise.

Legislators at both the state and federal levels appear to be considering increased regulation of these two very expensive sources of credit for individuals.

I have already mentioned credit card borrowing as another very high-cost source of credit, a cost that typically increases as the balance grows and if minimum monthly payments are not made on schedule. Even so, more than just a few entrepreneurs claim (perhaps with some exaggeration) that they started their small businesses by "maxing out," as it is often called, one or more of their credit cards.

Comparing the costs and benefits of various credit cards on offer can be quite a challenge, as many offer special side benefits. Some charge an annual fee; others don't. Some offered by airlines award miles based upon amounts charged to the card—the accumulation of award miles leads to future free flights. Others provide the holder with preferential boarding of flights. Some credit cards (e.g., one issued by Amazon) offer the holder 2 percent cash back on all purchases (3 percent on purchases from Amazon.)

Many credit card holders arrange for monthly payment of the full outstanding balance each month by direct deduction from their bank accounts. This is a foolproof way of avoiding high interest charges, but it does require that the holder have an adequate bank account balance on the payment due date.

> **Delinquency:** A loan is delinquent when required payments are not made on schedule.

To repeat, these credit sources are so expensive simply because the delinquency and default rates are so high. And bill-collecting—chasing after payment—is very expensive for the credit card companies!

> **Default:** A loan is in default when the borrower has ceased making the required payments.

Automobile Loans

The purchase of an automobile demands the second largest outlay of funds for many people, exceeded only by home purchases. And thus, many people borrow a major portion of the auto's purchase price. Indeed, most auto dealers apparently assume that few buyers can come up with the full purchase price in cash. Accordingly, they don't advertise the full price, but rather the monthly payment required to obtain the car. And much of this advertising is wildly misleading.

> **Auto Loans:** Loans made to automobile buyers; the value of the automobile serves as collateral—that is, security—for the borrowing.

As in financing a home purchase, a sizeable cash down payment is typically required when taking out an auto loan. Banks, credit unions, and other financial institutions provide auto loans. Car dealers themselves advertise that they will lend the funds to

Refinancing:
Occurs when the lender (for example, an auto dealer) contracts with a financial institution to take over a loan. Individual borrowers may also refinance a loan (for example, a home mortgage) to achieve additional borrowing, lower interest rates, extend time-to-maturity, or other loan term revisions.

Repossession:
The act by a lender to of taking back the collateral—say a car or a home—for a loan on which the borrower has ceased making payments (defaulted).

Collateral: The asset(s) that secure a loan and can be repossessed by the lender if and when the borrower defaults.

Installment loans:
Modest-size loans that are repaid over just a few years by regular (typically monthly) installment payments.

buyers, but in virtually all cases these dealers turn around and refinance this lending through a financial institution.

To stimulate the sale of new cars (perhaps to clear out inventory at model year-end), auto manufacturers and/or auto dealers from time to time advertise that they will loan to qualified car buyers at a very low interest rate, sometimes at zero interest. Are any of these organizations—manufacturer or dealer—really willing to lend to buyers and earn no interest? The simple answer is no. The "zero interest" come-on is simply a purchase price discount dressed up in a way that the manufacturer or dealer hopes will be more attractive to the buyer. That is, the buyer's monthly payment may be calculated assuming no interest, but when the dealer refinances this loan through a traditional financial institution, the institution will return to the dealer somewhat less than the loaned amount. This refinancing discount is, in effect, the dealer's price discount.

Therefore a car buyer may have difficulty figuring out what the true interest on a car loan is when the loan is negotiated through a dealer. The effective interest is generally in the "low teens"— say, 12 or 13 percent. Note that this rate is higher than interest rates on mortgages because (a) repossession and resale of a car is generally more difficult and uncertain than repossession and resale of a home, and (b) borrowers will default on car loans before they will default on their home mortgages. But the interest rate is also lower than that on credit card borrowing because (a) the default rate on car loans is lower, and (b) there is no collateral to repossess to satisfy a credit card loan default.

Many of us would be wise to consider foregoing the purchase of a new car—or home appliance or new furniture—for a few months or more while we accumulate sufficient funds to permit us to borrow at a more favorable interest rate or even to pay the full price in cash. There is no reason that each of us needs to adopt the apparent American culture of "paying for all major purchases in installments." In fact, by saving the interest charges, we can actually buy more over the long term.

Installment Loans

Installment loans are often used for the purchase of "big ticket" items such as appliances, household furnishings, home entertainment systems, and recreational equipment. These loans tend to carry higher interest rates than auto loans, in part because repossession of these purchases is more difficult and resale of the repossessed item is less likely to recoup the remaining outstanding loan balance.

Insurance premiums, college tuitions, and many other purchases can be paid for over time (i.e., in installments.) A little "sharp pencil" work, employing the ideas and interest tables discussed in chapter 3, can quickly convince one that the inherent interest rates are high.

Home Mortgages

Nonetheless, you are unlikely to be able to save sufficient amounts for a long enough period of time to pay cash for your first home—unless of course you get major financial help from a rich uncle or parent! Thus, you will negotiate (or have negotiated) a home mortgage contract. The collateral for the mortgage is, of course, the home itself. Conventional mortgages specify an interest rate and a term; monthly payments throughout the term are sufficient to cover the interest on the loan and to repay the principal over the term of the mortgage (say, twenty or thirty years.)

Home mortgage: A loan for which the home itself serves as collateral

The monthly mortgage payment remains constant throughout the term of the mortgage. In the early years of the mortgage, when the loan amount outstanding (i.e., the remaining principal balance) is high, most of the monthly mortgage payment must be devoted to the interest expense, and the small remainder to principal reduction. However, as the outstanding principal is reduced, the interest charge falls, as it is based on the size of the outstanding balance. Therefore, late in the term of the mortgage, the reverse is the case: the principal balance now outstanding is low, thus the interest expense is low. Accordingly, a large share of the monthly mortgage payment is devoted to reduction of the principal balance. For this reason, many homeowners, having made monthly mortgage payments for ten years on a thirty-year mortgage (one-third of the term), are surprised that the principal reduction has been reduced by much less than one-third.

The rate of interest charged by the lender reflects that lender's assessment of the riskiness of the loan. (That truism, by the way, applies to all lending, not just home mortgages.) If the buyer is able to make a down payment equivalent to, say, 25 percent of the purchase price of the home, he or she will receive a more favorable interest rate than another buyer who can come up with only a 10 percent down payment. Home buyers who can demonstrate that their earnings will cover the monthly mortgage payment with ease—or buyers who have significant portfolios of other assets or have little or no other outstanding debt—will receive more favorable home loan interest rates than others whose living expenses and debt commitments stretch their income to the limit.

Second Mortgage: Provides additional funds for the borrower to use in purchasing a home. The lender has a "second" call on the collateral to satisfy its loan; the first call on the collateral goes to the lender of the first mortgage.

Some buyers require more than one loan to purchase the home— that is, both a first and a second mortgage, often from different lenders. The financial institution providing the second mortgage is taking a substantially greater risk—and thus will charge a higher interest rate—than the "first" mortgage lender, since, in the event of default and repossession, the first loan must be satisfied before the "second" lender receives anything.

Monthly mortgage payments are typically made from the borrower's monthly income. A widely quoted rule of thumb is that the mortgage payments should not exceed 30 percent of the homeowner's income. When the payments exceed that threshold, the borrower has probably overinvested in residential property.

Once upon a time, commercial banks were the primary negotiators of home loans, and held the loans until they were fully repaid by the homeowner. In recent decades, this market has become highly fragmented, with mortgage brokers initiating the process, banks providing the funds at the outset but then "selling" the loans to others engaged one way or another in the credit markets; more about this later.

Mortgage lenders may impose other fees on the homebuyer at the time the mortgage is originated or paid off. These fees serve to increase the effective mortgage interest rate.

Government Involvement in the Mortgage Market

The federal government has been a major player in the home mortgage market. A rationale for this involvement is that home ownership is "part of the American Dream" and widespread ownership leads to a more responsible and stable citizenry.

First, home mortgage interest paid on the borrower's primary residence is deductible (with some limitations) for income tax purposes, thus lowering the after-tax cost of home ownership. For example, a homeowner with a 30 percent marginal income tax rate and a 6 percent home mortgage interest rate has an after-tax interest rate on the mortgage of 4.2 percent.

This tax benefit needs to be kept in perspective—any borrowing, even when their home is the collateral, adds to owners' debt leverage and thus increases their financial risk. This risk caused many people to lose their homes (that is, lenders foreclosed on and repossessed many homes) when, in 2008–2010 a serious economic recession coincided with—and/or caused—a sharp decline in home prices. Widespread repossessions by lenders, who then tried to resell the properties, put further downward pressure on home prices.

A second governmental involvement in the home mortgage market occurs through the actions of two quasi-governmental firms established to further boost home ownership: Fannie Mae and Freddie Mac. These are public-private firms, operating (more or less) as independent commercial operations but with access to borrowing at preferential federal government interest rates to fund their mortgages.

During the housing boom of 2002–2007, Fannie and Freddie got carried away—as did the rest of the mortgage industry—lending too aggressively and without adequate controls. As a result, the federal government had to rescue these two firms, which now operate much more like federal agencies than independent companies. They continue to provide a large percentage of the funding for home mortgages.

Nonconventional Mortgages

The previous section has focused on what might be called conventional or traditional mortgages. But many mortgage variations exist in the mortgage market place. Some provide for a variation in interest rates as conditions change in the credit markets. Some provide for lower monthly payments for a few years (a "teaser" rate), followed by a step-up. Some lenders, apparently projecting that home prices would increase forever, entered interest-only mortgages: the monthly payments did not reduce the principal balance of the mortgage.

Reverse mortgages have also increased in popularity for elderly homeowners whose homes are (a) their primary (or sole) asset,

After-tax interest rate: The borrowing rate after giving effect to the tax deductibility of part or all of the associated interest expense.

Foreclosure: The termination of a lending agreement by the lender because of default by the buyer. Repossession of the associated collateral typically follows foreclosure.

Reverse Mortgages: May be available to elderly persons who have no mortgage on their homes. These individuals can borrow each month for living expenses, with the result that the "mortgage" increases each month. The home is the collateral for the mortgage that is ultimately repaid from the proceeds of the sale of the home (typically upon the death of the borrower).

and (b) no longer subject to mortgage. The "reverse" works as follows: the person(s) needing extra income to cover living expenses during retirement borrows each month; the mortgage balance thus increases (rather than decreases) each month as more is borrowed and interest in accrued; and the mortgage obligation is paid off from the sale of the home upon the death of the owners/borrowers. If the elderly homeowners' life expectancies are estimated conservatively (that is, long life is assumed in calculating the terms of the reverse mortgage), these mortgages involve relatively low risk to either the lender or the borrower.

Cosigning on Individual Borrowing

You may from time-to-time be asked by friends or family members to "cosign a note"—a bank borrowing, a car loan, or a mortgage. Beware! Acceding to what may seem like an innocuous request puts you fully liable for the borrowing, should your friend or family member be unable to meet its terms for the payment of interest and repayment of principle. The lender will not hesitate to come after you!

Review Questions for Chapter 4:

1. Why would a person take out a payday loan, since he or she must know that this is a very expensive source of funds?
2. Why has the federal government become so deeply involved in the home mortgage market?
3. What is the logic behind the rule of thumb that monthly mortgage payments should be kept below about 30 percent of monthly income? In the last decade or so, many people violated this rule of thumb quite substantially. What motivated them to do so?
4. Consider various forms of collateral owned by a borrower: shares of common stock, cars, precious jewelry, home, speed boat, family heirlooms, furniture and kitchen appliances. What are the characteristics of assets that prove most useful as loan collateral?
5. In about 2010, repossession of homes (because of defaults on mortgages) was said to cause a downward spiral of home prices. Why?
6. Suppose a homeowner ceases making monthly mortgage payments because the market value of her home has declined to less than the outstanding mortgage balance. What possible courses of action might the lender take?

Chapter Five

CORPORATIONS

Corporation: an artificial entity that can do everything but make love.

—Anonymous

At this juncture, we need to understand a bit more about <u>corporations</u>. Most of us end up both working for corporations and at some point investing in their shares of common stock.

Corporations: The Dominant Form of Organization

Most corporations are profit seeking—that is, they try hard to earn profits. But most nonprofits are also corporations: private schools and colleges, social service agencies, museums, art performing groups, and so forth. Corporations are so-called legal entities: they can sue and be sued, just as can individuals. They are separate and distinct from the individuals who own the corporation's common shares. A corporation can be owned by thousands—even millions—of shareholders. At the other extreme, a single individual may own all the shares of the corporation. A corporation has a perpetual life: it exists until it is formally dissolved.

Corporate entities are <u>incorporated</u>—licensed, if you will—by a state, not necessarily the state in which they do most or all of their business. The process of incorporation is straightforward, typically neither lengthy nor expensive.

A corporation is governed by its board of directors ("the board"), and the shareholders elect the directors, generally annually. The

<u>Corporation:</u> A legal entity separate and distinct from its owner, created by action of one of the fifty states, in response to a petition by its existing or potential owners.

<u>Incorporation:</u> The incorporation of a for-profit or nonprofit entity results from formal action by a state.

<u>Board of Directors:</u> The governing board of a corporation, with its members elected by the corporation's owners—or otherwise appointed in the case of non-profit corporations.

board appoints the officers (president, vice presidents, treasurer, and so forth). It also makes decisions regarding, for example, (a) the mission and strategy of the company, (b) its financing, and (c) the appointment of independent auditors to review the corporation's financial statements. The Board is typically comprised of both "insiders," people who work for the company, and "independents," those who are not employed by the company. The mix of insider and independent directors varies widely among corporations. Large corporations typically have a large majority of independent members of their boards. Typically, independent directors are compensated, while insiders simply receive their corporate salaries.

Shareholders and others occasionally sue directors; the charges typically allege illegal corporate actions or actions that are not in the best interests of the shareholders. This exposure to risk is a major reason why directors should take their responsibilities seriously and expect to be reasonably well compensated.

As you undoubtedly already know, the federal government (the Internal Revenue Service) taxes corporate profits, as do most foreign governments of countries where the corporation has business activities, and state governments where the corporation has business activities. The corporate tax rate schedule is separate from the personal income tax schedule.

Corporate Net Worth

Recall the discussion in chapter 2 of the net worth of individuals. The formula "Net Worth = Assets – Obligations" applies as well to corporations as to individuals. Assets are pretty straight forward: cash in the bank and on hand; amounts due from customers (called <u>accounts receivable</u>); inventories of all kinds; property, plant and equipment owned by the corporation (called <u>fixed assets</u>); and <u>intangible assets</u> such as patents, license arrangements, and so forth.

Obligations consist of both liabilities and, surprisingly, net worth. First liabilities: amounts owed to suppliers (called <u>accounts payable</u>), amounts owed to employees (i.e., wages and salaries earned but not yet paid), borrowings from banks and from others that remain outstanding, taxes owed but not yet paid, and so forth.

Accounts Receivable: Amounts owed by the corporation's customers.

Fixed Assets: Property, plant, and equipment owned by the corporation.

Intangible Assets: Typically intellectual properties such as patents that are owned by the corporation.

Accounts Payable: Amount owed to suppliers and other contractors.

Corporations are also obligated to their shareholders. Thus, corporate net worth is a "plus" for its shareholders, but an obligation for the corporation itself. The corporation has an obligation to use shareholders' funds entrusted to it to earn returns (in one form or another) for its shareholders. Thus, corporate net worth is the sum of (a) the amounts invested by shareholders as, from time to time, the corporation sells newly issued shares; and (b) net profits earned by the corporation and not paid out as <u>dividends</u> but rather reinvested in assets of the corporation.

<u>Dividends:</u> Periodic cash payments—a set amount per share—by a corporation to its shareholders.

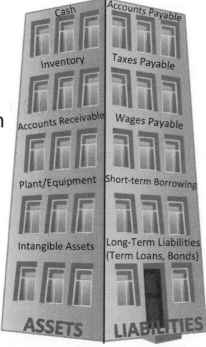

Corporate Net Worth

A corporation is, of course, required to pay interest and principal on borrowings in accordance with the terms of its agreement with the lender; failure to do so represents a default on the loan, and defaults can lead to bankruptcy. By contrast, corporations are not required to pay dividends of any stated amount at any particular time. Dividends are paid at the discretion of the board of directors; if the board feels that the corporation has insufficient cash to pay dividends or has profitable uses of the cash (investing in its business operations), it may elect to forego the payment of dividends for a short or long period of time. Failure to pay dividends cannot result in a default.

Bear in mind that transactions among shareholders—that is, buying and selling (trading) common stock—does not involve the corporation; the corporation whose stock is being traded is not a party to the transaction. Accordingly, these trades do not affect corporate net worth.

Commercial Bank: A traditional financial institution that accepts deposits and pays interest on certain of these deposits; redeems withdrawals from such accounts – that is, depositors' checks; and makes loans.

A figure in chapter 2 outlines the components of individuals' net worth. That figure is expanded upon here to illustrate typical components of corporate net worth. Further on in this chapter another figure will show the components of net worth for typical commercial banks.

Corporate Income Taxes

Corporate annual earnings are subject to tax in accordance with a tax schedule separate from that applicable to individuals. Like the personal tax schedule, it provides for graduated rates.

Income tax rules for both individuals and corporations are voluminous and they seem to grow more complicated year by year. Here are a few provisions that are particularly relevant to our discussion:

a. Interest payments on corporate debt are tax deductible; dividend payments to the corporation's shareholders are not.
b. Expenses are, of course, deductible, but expenditures to acquire assets with multiyear lives are not deductible; these assets must be depreciated. (See next section of this chapter.)
c. Earnings generated in foreign countries may or may not be taxed by the U.S. government, depending upon the disposition of the earnings.
d. Operating losses may be "carried back" to recoup some taxes paid in previous years and/or carried forward to offset future years' taxes.

Valuation

In the discussion of individual net worth, the subject of valuation was raised. We need now to look more deeply into the valuation issue as it relates to corporate net worth.

Repeating from chapter 2: Any error in valuation of an asset or a liability will necessarily result in an error in the valuation of net worth, since net worth is, in effect, a derived number.

Valuations are often—and necessarily—based on estimates because firm data are not readily available. For example, how can one precisely value a five-year old machine tool with an undetermined remaining life; or a customer's promise to pay if it is known that the customer is experiencing financial difficulty; or an inventory item that may or may not prove of interest to customers? In each of these cases, accounting rules instruct corporations how they should value these and other assets. For example:

a. Fixed assets such as machine tools are <u>depreciated</u>: their values are reduced from their original cost over the expected useful life of the fixed asset. Of course, the estimate of useful life may turn out to be incorrect.

b. Accounts receivable are valued by deducting an estimate of the amount that will ultimately prove uncollectible. Note that this is a statistical approach to valuation, not a specific identification of customers who will or won't pay.

c. An approach similar to that used for accounts receivable valuation is used for inventory valuation. Almost inevitably, certain inventory items will not sell or will otherwise prove to be useless. Again, a statistical approach is used, one honed by the historical experience of the owner of the inventory, to arrive at an estimate of inventory value.

> **Depreciation:** The allocation of the cost of assets to periods in which the assets are used. Incidentally, these depreciation expenses are typically tax deductible to the corporation.

Moreover, from time to time, accounting rule makers change the valuation rules on certain assets and liabilities. For example, until about a decade ago most monetary assets and liabilities were valued at what would be received or paid by the owner at maturity (i.e., when due.) Now many of these assets must be valued at their current market value, in a process known as <u>marking-to-market</u>.

> **Marking-to-Market:** Requires that monetary assets and liabilities be valued at the price they could be sold or bought for in the markets.

Why is marking-to-market sometimes important? Consider the housing price "bust" in 2007–2010, when many owners ceased making payments on their mortgages because either (a) they bought more expensive houses than they could afford, believing that house prices "always" increase; or (b) they found it foolish to continue to pay on a mortgage the balance of which exceeded their home's current market value. To value more reasonably the mortgages they held, the lenders were forced to mark-to-market; thus, their loan assets and therefore their net worths were reduced substantially.

Valuation is also challenging for global corporations who do business is many different countries, and therefore in different currencies. Suppose the Witte Corporation based in the United States has customers in France who pay in euros and in Japan who pay in yen. Obviously, Witte cannot value its accounts receivable from this diverse set of customers by adding together U.S. dollars, euros, and Japanese yen. Because the company is based in the United States, Witte almost surely maintains its accounting records in U.S. dollars. Therefore, in valuing its total accounts receivable, it needs to convert the euros receivables into U.S. dollars, using the prevailing exchange rate between the two currencies; similarly, it converts yen receivables to dollar equivalents. Note that these conversions (for financial reporting purposes) do not change the fact that Witte's French customers will remit euros and the Japanese customers will remit yen.

Presumably, Witte has bank accounts in France and Japan where it can deposit these remittances as received. Witte will then decide whether it has uses for euros—for example, to invest in several of its European operations, or to make payments to its suppliers and employees in Europe; or should the euros be exchanged for U.S. dollars, and these dollars brought back to U.S. headquarters.

Note, thus, that global companies can gain earnings—or lose earnings—as exchange rates fluctuate. Various financial transactions (called hedging, which will be discussed further in chapter 8) can mitigate these gains and losses.

Commercial Banks: A Special Corporate Case

Because both individuals as well as industrial and commercial corporations have extensive interactions with commercial banks, let's spend a minute considering the activities and typical net worths of this subset of corporations.

In simplest terms, a commercial bank does the following: it accepts deposits from, and honors the withdrawals by, its deposit customers. Because the bank has an obligation to pay out depositors' funds "upon demand" (they are called "demand deposits"), these balances are liabilities of the commercial bank. The bank then lends most of the cash provided by depositors to individual and corporate borrowers. Because borrowers are obligated to pay back these loans, they are the primary assets of the commercial bank.

If this seems backward to you, that is probably because you are thinking of "deposits" and "loans" from your own viewpoint; indeed, they are, respectively, assets and liabilities to you, but they are just the opposite to the bank. So it is worth reminding ourselves that an asset for one corporation or individual may be a liability of another; that "other" is referred to as the <u>counterparty</u>.

The table below also shows the components of the assets, liabilities and net worth of typical commercial banks. Incidentally, investment banks have different functions than commercial banks; they are discussed in chapter 7.

Bear in mind too, that commercial banks are subject to a great deal of regulation, both federal and state. This regulation is aimed primarily at protecting bank customers from losing their deposits.

Counterparty: The individual or entity that is on the other side of a transaction. If one sells an asset to another, that buyer is the counterparty to the seller.

Debt Leverage: Corporations

Debt leverage—both positive and negative—works similarly for corporations as it does for individuals. That is, a corporation in most any industry has two primary sources of capital for investing in its operations: funds provided by its shareholders and funds it borrows from various credit sources (think first of banks; we will review other sources in subsequent chapters). Remember that shareholder capital comes to the corporation in two ways: (1) shareholders purchase shares newly issued by the corporation; and (2) <u>retained earnings</u>: net profits of the corporation that have not been paid out in the form of dividends, but have rather been reinvested in the corporation (for the future benefit of shareholders).

Retained earnings: Corporate net profits that have not – or at least not yet – been paid out to shareholders in the form of dividends.

As we will see in a subsequent chapter, investors anticipate that over time, their returns from stock investments will be greater than from <u>corporate bonds</u> (that is, bond investments, discussed in chapter 6). Why? To compensate them for the added risks they assume through stock ownership by comparison with bond ownership. Should the corporation get into financial trouble the creditors (bond holders) have claims on the corporation that take precedence over shareholder claims: creditors must be paid interest and debt repayment before shareholders are paid.

Corporate bond: A negotiable financial certificate that acknowledges the indebtedness of the corporation issuing the bond to the current bond owner (investor).

Thus, typically the cost to the corporation of obtaining funds from shareholders is higher than the cost of borrowing money— but so also are the risks to the corporation (and thus to its owners—that is, its shareholders.) If, say, a corporation needs $200 million for a promising investment, it might borrow part of the funds and obtain the rest from shareholders (retained earnings or newly issued stock.) Then if the returns from this investment exceed the cost of the borrowed funds—and that surely is the corporate management's expectation at the time it borrows and invests—the corporation, and thus, its shareholders will benefit from this positive leverage.

As with individuals, some corporations are willing to accept the risks associated with high debt leverage. Some have borrowings equal to two or more times the funds supplied by the shareholders. And if the basic business of the corporation is not very risky, this debt policy may be wholly appropriate.

On the other hand, other corporations who want to minimize their financing risk will minimize their borrowings. The CEO of one successful technology company once stated, "Our company does not borrow money." period! He was saying that the corporation willingly passes up the potential benefits of positive leverage in order to minimize its financing risk. Presumably, the board of directors, the management, and the shareholders were satisfied with that trade-off. (Of course, if the shareholders are not satisfied, they can always sell their shares and invest elsewhere.)

An old question asked by corporate treasurers is, "Would you rather sleep well"—forego the risks, and also the potential of leveraged returns, "or eat well?"—seek to capture the benefits of debt leverage and accept the attendant risks.

Here is a look at how the Walt Disney Company finances its operations. At the end of 2011, its total assets were $72.1 billion. Remember that, accordingly, the sum of its liabilities and net worth – the sources of its funding – must also be $72.1 billion. Disney's net worth was $39.4 billion, and thus, its liabilities were $32.7 billion, comprised of:

Short-term liabilities	$12.1
Borrowings	$10.9
Other long-term liabilities	$19.7

Disney's financial statements reveal that for the year 2011, interest expenses on its borrowings were $332 million. Thus, the interest rate on its $10.9 million of borrowing was about 3 percent. Disney's earnings were 11.2 percent of its total assets. When Disney can borrow at 3 percent to invest in assets that earn 11.2 percent, the company and its shareholders are enjoying positive debt leverage.

Could Disney borrow more and then pay higher dividends to its shareholders; that is, could it undertake additional debt leverage? Yes, it probably could, but presumably its Board of Directors has determined not to subject the company to the higher risk associated with greater borrowing, particularly since the business of film and television production, Disney's main activities, is inherently risky.

Bank Leverage

Banks typically operate with very high debt leverage. From whom are they borrowing? Primarily their depositors; as noted earlier in this chapter, deposits are by far and away banks' major liabilities.

To repeat: banks promise depositors they can withdraw funds from their checking accounts at essentially any time, in any amount. In normal times, that promise is not risky because the bank has many, many depositors and no single depositor's funds represent more than a small fraction of the liabilities (deposits) of the bank. A well-run bank is able to forecast total deposits and withdrawals with considerable accuracy and thus be prepared to meet its obligations.

But suppose a borrower becomes bankrupt and thus is unlikely ever to repay his outstanding loan. What is the impact on the bank's finances? The value of the asset, "loans receivable," declines by the amount of the "write off" of the defaulted loan; deposits are unaffected; and thus, the bank's net worth declines by the amount of the default.

The dangers arise when the bank encounters abnormal times—say, a recession, a depression, a stock market slump, or widespread failure of a certain agricultural crop. Not only do more loans turn sour, but also bank withdrawals may skyrocket, with the result that the bank is unable to keep its promise to the remaining depositors. And if a warning (or even rumor) spreads that a certain bank may not be able to make good on its depositors' withdrawal demands, a "run" on the bank commences: depositors run to the bank in hopes of getting their funds out before others do and before the bank fails. This scenario is the one that faced Greek and Spanish banks in mid-2012.

These were also common occurrences in the depression of the 1930s and again in the deep recession and housing slump toward the end of the first decade of the current century. In 2008–2009 the U.S. federal government loaned massive amounts to banks to assure that these banks had sufficient liquidity to meet their obligations; had they not done so, more than just a few of these banks would have failed, deepening the economic recession that was already severe.

Subsequent to the 1930s depression, many actions have been taken to safeguard individual depositors. First, bank regulations and inspections were stepped up substantially. Second, the federal government commenced an insurance operation—Federal Deposit Insurance Corporation (FDIC)—to which banks make insurance premium payments and the FDIC, in turn, stands ready to take over failing banks and assure full repayment (up to a certain high limit) of deposits to its customers.

Banks may operate with debt leverages of, say, 20–1. That is, deposits (and other liabilities) are twenty times as great as net worth. As we saw above, banks' primary assets are loans: loans of all kinds including home mortgages, loans to operating businesses, and auto loans. Just as no single depositor carries a balance that represents a significant share of the bank's total liabilities, no single loan represents a significant share of its assets. If you will, the "rule of large numbers" (diversification) is at work.

But suppose a small, rural bank has a large percentage of loans to farmers in its regions, most growing the same one or two agriculture crops. If the weather in a particular year causes widespread crop failure, the bank's loan default rate may escalate. Thus, the bank may get into financial trouble even though no single farmer's borrowing is particularly large. The bank may be diversified in terms of individual farmers, but not in terms of the source of repayment of the loans, that is, not diversified as to agricultural crop.

Similarly, in 2008–2010 many banks found themselves in trouble because they overrelied on home mortgage lending and failed to diversify those loans geographically. Where inexpensive housing was overbuilt—for example, in Nevada, Arizona, and Florida—banks found themselves having to repossess homes from owner/borrowers who defaulted on their mortgages. But by then the slump in home prices in those regions had driven the value of the homes well below the outstanding balances on the home mortgages. Many banks and related financial institutions failed.

Nevertheless, profitable commercial bank operation requires the use of leverage: loan totals much greater than the bank's net worth. A widely used measure of the extent of leverage is the bank's "loan-to-deposit" ratio: the total dollar value of outstanding loans—its primary asset—divided by the total dollar value of today's deposits—its primary liability. Generally, that ratio is below 1.0; loans do not exceed deposits.

Corporate Borrowing

Traditional bank borrowing by industrial and commercial corporations is in the form of lines-of-credit or term loans. A few words about each:

Short-Term Borrowing

Line-of-credit: Provides the corporation, in effect, an option to borrow funds up to a certain limit over a defined, short time period.

A corporation regularly arranges a line-of-credit with one or more commercial banks that permit it to borrow and repay at any time amounts up to a certain maximum. Two typical examples: a retailer may use a line-of-credit to acquire merchandise in advance of its busy season—the year-end holidays or, for a sports store, the summer season—and repay part or all of the borrowing from the proceeds of the sale of the merchandise; an industrial company may find that the pattern of its sales and of customer payments causes it to run short of cash from time to time. A line-of-credit tides the borrower over these times.

Often these lines-of-credit provide that the maximum that can be borrowed at any one time shall be not greater than a certain percentage (say, 75 or 80 percent) of the borrower's accounts receivable, the corporation's most liquid asset other than cash. Moreover, the loan agreement may further provide that, should the borrower be unable to repay, the lender may "seize" (the legal term) the accounts receivable and notify customers to remit directly to the bank rather than to the borrower. Obviously, such seizures are catastrophic events for borrowers.

Collateral is the term used to refer to the asset pledged (formally or informally) to the lender as "security" for borrowing. While accounts receivable are the most common form of collateral, they are not the only one. Some types of inventory may also serve as attractive collateral: gold for a jewelry manufacturer; standard forms of intermediate steel products for a steel fabricator; and raw agricultural products for a food processor. The key, of course, is that the inventory must be readily resalable at a reasonable price in the event the lender has to seize it.

Term Loans

Term loans typically call for repayment of principal over the next few years—say, five or seven. Such loans are often negotiated to permit the borrower to make a certain capital investment (e.g., machinery) or acquire another company whose business is related. In either of these examples, the expectation typically is that the earnings (or cost savings) derived from the investment will be sufficient to repay the term loan in compliance with the loan agreement's provisions.

As is the case with lines-of-credit, these term loans may be either secured (by specific pledges of collateral) or unsecured.

Term Loans:
Corporate term loans typically specify (a) the amount borrowed, (b) the final maturity (the term) of the loan, (c) the interest rate, (d) the required repayment installments, and (e) miscellaneous other provisions.

Secured Loans:
Loans that specify the collateral that may be seized (sold) should the borrower default on the loan.

59

Fixed interest rates: Remain constant throughout the term of the loan, regardless of changed conditions in the credit markets.

Floating interest rates: Change as prevailing interest rates increase or decrease.

Prime Rate: The interest rate charged by banks to their most credit-worthy customers.

Bond Indenture: The extensive legal document that spells all of the terms between the issuing corporation and the investor in (buyer of) the bond.

Lessor: Equivalent to the "lender" in a lease transaction, except that the lessor actually owns the physical asset being leased, thus simplifying repossession should that be necessary.

Lessee: equivalent to the "borrower" in a lease transaction.

Floating and Fixed Interest Rates

A credit agreement between lender and borrower may provide for a <u>fixed</u> interest rate—the same interest rate throughout the term of the loan. Others may provide for a so-called <u>floating rate</u> that will vary as overall credit conditions vary. For example, a line-of-credit may provide for an interest rate that is 0.5 percent above the so-called <u>prime rate</u>: the rate charged by lenders to their most credit-worthy clients. The prime rate goes up or down depending on the availability of credit (supply of lendable funds), forecasts of economic activity (loan demand), and expected inflation.

Selling Bonds in the Public Market

Corporations can also borrow by selling bonds in the public market. Typically, this option is open only to medium-sized and large corporations, as the costs associated with such sales can only be justified by raising substantial sums. When corporations sell bonds, they are entering into long-term borrowing arrangements with those institutions or individuals who "purchase" the bonds. The terms of this borrowing are spelled out in great detail in the so-called <u>bond indenture</u>. In recent years many corporate bonds have involved creative and complicated terms that are well beyond the scope of this book. But some further discussion appears in chapter 7, "Public Credit Markets."

Mortgages and Leases

As individuals may negotiate mortgages to buy homes, corporations may enter similar arrangements to acquire real estate for use in their businesses. For corporations whose business is developing and/or leasing residential, industrial, or commercial properties, mortgages are a major financing source. Leases of equipment or real estate are analogous to term loans, except that the <u>lessor</u> (lender) rather than the <u>lessee</u> (borrower) retains ownership of the asset throughout the term of the lease. Frequently income tax considerations render a lease more advantageous than a term loan to both "lender" and "borrower."

Bear in mind that leases are different from short-term rental agreements of, for example, information technology equipment such as copiers, computers, and so forth.. First, the term of the lease (during which the lessee may not cancel the contract) is often equal to (or nearly so) the useful life of the asset (say, a vehicle, or a machine tool). A rental agreement is generally of shorter duration, and may be cancelable by the renter on short notice.

Personal Guarantees

Lenders to smaller corporations often request the personal guarantee of the primary owner(s) of the business and/or one or more of its senior officers. Personal guarantees are the equivalent of "cosigning" on a personal debt, as discussed in chapter 4. Beware!

Mergers and Acquisitions

Corporate entities are combined with some frequency, either by merger or by acquisition. These combinations are generally intended to provide operating efficiencies for the combined companies. However, objective studies of corporate combinations over the past several decades seem to conclude that most combinations were not successful—that is, the combinations were not beneficial for the shareholders.

An acquiring company pays for an acquisition by paying the shareholders of the acquired company either cash (so much per share), newly issued shares of the acquiring company, or some combination of the two.

Corporate Bankruptcy

As with individuals, corporations (including financial institutions) sometimes go bankrupt. A negative net worth may foretell possible bankruptcy, but this condition does not automatically result in bankruptcy. In brief, a corporation's creditors may force bankruptcy proceedings against a corporation that is in financial difficulty, or the corporation may seek "voluntary" bankruptcy. In either case, the courts step in to protect the corporation from harassment by its creditors while attempting to work out the best mutual arrangement for both debtor and creditors. Bankruptcy proceedings may result in liquidation of the corporation: selling the corporation's assets at the best possible price and using the proceeds to repay creditors to the extent possible. In "voluntary" cases, typically called a chapter 11 bankruptcy, the court may permit the corporation to operate, subject to a plan of reorganization that typically requires some restructuring of the corporation: perhaps new management, perhaps the sale or suspension of certain underperforming lines of business.

Recall that in 2008 two of the three large U.S. automobile manufacturers went bankrupt. When these companies were able to shed certain obligations and attract "bailout" investments from the federal government, the courts permitted these companies to continue operating. To date, the joint decisions of the federal government, the courts, and the automobile companies seem to have been wise ones.

Most of the large U.S. commercial airlines have declared bankruptcy at least once, and some have continued to operate for years under the protection of bankruptcy.

Recently, Borders Books went bankrupt and was unable to work out a satisfactory restructuring or to attract new investors; the court and the company finally determined that liquidation provided the best outcome for the creditors, although they did not receive 100 percent of amounts owed to them by Borders.

Review Questions for Chapter 5:

1. Financial returns come to corporate shareholders in two forms; one is dividends. What is the other possible form of return?
2. Why might a corporation seek voluntary bankruptcy (that is, without being forced by its creditors)?
3. Explain why deposits in a bank are considered liabilities for the bank.
4. Under what conditions might a corporate borrower prefer a fixed interest rate, rather than a floating rate?
5. What are the advantages to a corporation of leasing facilities or equipment rather than purchasing them?
6. Explain why "accounts receivable" are a corporation's most likely collateral to secure short-term borrowing.
7. Why are commercial banks able to operate successfully with debt leverage much higher than is possible for manufacturing corporations?
8. What are the primary differences between a rental and a lease agreement?
9. Why does the bankruptcy court sometimes permit a bankrupt company to continue to operate?

Chapter Six

PUBLIC CREDIT MARKETS

The lifeblood of commerce.

—Elbert Hubbard

A condition of human relationships, it binds the future to the present by the confidence we have in the integrity of those with whom we deal.

—James T. Shotwell

Governmental units—federal, state, and municipal—borrow funds "in the public market." That is, from time to time, they sell bonds, typically in very large dollar amounts, with one or more specified due dates (when the borrowing is to be repaid), a stated interest rate, and typically a requirement that interest be paid semiannually.

As discussed in the last chapter, large corporations also may, from time to time, issue bonds—that is, borrow in the public market. Presumably, the directors of the issuing corporation feel that utilizing this additional debt to grow and enhance its business (perhaps, for example, to make corporate acquisitions) will result in positive leverage for its shareholders. Some corporate bonds are secured by certain of the corporation's assets; other bonds are unsecured.

Trading in Credit Markets

The general public—that is, you and I—are welcome to buy government and corporate bonds when they are issued. However, the greater demand for these debt instruments comes from institutions: banks, insurance companies, mutual funds (to be discussed in a subsequent chapter), pension funds, endowment funds, and others who are prepared to commit large sums to these investments.

Once issued, these bonds trade—that is, they are bought and sold—in organized markets. Again, you and I are welcome to trade. A pension fund that owns government bonds may need to sell some of them to raise funds to meet its other obligations (making payments to pensioners, for example), or simply because it believes certain other securities available in the markets represent more attractive investments, given the objectives of the pension fund.

Purchases and sales of previously issued bonds—issued by governmental units or corporations—do not involve the issuer. They are simply negotiated between buyer and seller, typically with the assistance of a broker (likely a Wall Street securities firm specializing in bond trading); the prices at which these bonds trade bear no necessary relationship to the price received initially by the issuing government unit or corporate entity.

Why do prices change? Because conditions in the credit markets change. And thus, prevailing interest rates increase and decrease (as discussed presently), and, of course, the financial strength (the credit worthiness) of the issuer also may increase or decrease.

Credit Quality and Bond Ratings

As the probability declines that a borrower will repay in full and on time, the credit-worthiness of the borrower—an individual, a corporation, a governmental unit—also declines. And the interest rate that the lender will charge the borrower increases.

Risk-free interest rate: The interest rate at which the Federal government can borrow for short time periods.

The so-called risk-free interest rate at any point in time is the rate that the U.S. federal government currently pays on its short-term borrowing; more accurately, the federal government's short-term interest rate is the closest the credit markets get to a truly risk-free rate. Except under very unusual circumstances and for very short periods of time, interest rates on all other borrowings by corporations or government units are higher than this risk-free rate. Given both (a) the size and growth rate of our federal debt and (b) the fact that in recent years a few countries have in fact defaulted on their debts, you might be surprised that lending to the federal government (that is, investing in its debt instruments) is considered to be essentially risk free.

The point is this: lending to all other borrowers is considered to be riskier than lending to the federal government.

64

Publicly traded bonds are generally <u>rated</u> as to credit-worthiness (riskiness) by independent, nongovernmental <u>rating agencies</u>. The three largest such agencies are Moody's, Standard and Poor's, and Fitch. Ratings range from AAA (referred to as "triple A") for the most credit-worthy, to B and C (with various "+'s" and "–'s" thrown in.) Bonds of still lesser credit-worthiness remain unrated. The corporation issuing the bonds pays fees to one or all three of the rating agencies for their services in rating.

These rating agencies failed utterly to foretell the credit crisis of 2008–2009 by changing the rating in a timely manner on corporate bonds, particularly those of financial institutions. As a result, a fair number of bonds went into default during this period, even as the rating agencies continued to rate them triple-A. The agencies and the bond markets learned some hard lessons!

Those bonds that are "unrated," or have very low ratings, have been tagged with the name <u>junk bonds</u>. These bonds, as you would imagine, must pay high interest rates to reward the investor for accepting the higher risk of default. Thus, the more polite name for junk bonds is <u>high-yield</u> bonds.

High-yield bonds play an important role in the financing of high-risk entities, both corporations and governmental units (more about them from an investor's viewpoint in a subsequent chapter).

Interaction of Price and Yield

Suppose that you are interested in buying $35,000 worth of bonds issued three years ago by the Phelps Corporation. The bonds are due (to be repaid) in seven years and bear an interest rate (so-called <u>coupon rate</u>) of 7 percent. Suppose further that the <u>prevailing interest rate</u> for bonds issued today, having a seven-year maturity by a corporation of credit-worthiness similar to Phelps's, is 8.5 percent. You correctly anticipate that Phelps's bonds now sell at a discount from their issuing price because interest rates have increased.

Why is this so? Because the potential purchaser of the outstanding Phelps bond has the option of buying another corporation's newly issued bond, comparable in "riskiness" and time-

---

<u>Rated:</u> Bonds of all types are rated (or they may remain unrated) by independent agents –

<u>Rating Agencies:</u> as to their current credit-worthiness and probable future credit-worthiness, that is, the risk that they will not be fully redeemed at maturity.

<u>High Yield (Junk) Bonds:</u> Those bonds that must offer investors high interest returns because of their riskiness.

<u>Coupon Rate:</u> The percentage of the stated value of the bond that will be paid annually to whomever then owns the bond.

<u>Prevailing Interest Rates:</u> The rates at which corporations of similar credit quality can borrow in the amount and for the time period indicated.

to-maturity as Phelps's; that bond will pay the buyer 8.5 percent annual interest. So the buyer won't be interested in Phelps's outstanding bonds unless they sell at a discount so that their coupon rate results in a higher return (called yield-to-maturity) on the now discounted price. Compound interest tables (based on the factors shown in appendix A of chapter 3) reveal to all who trade in the bond markets what discounted price would make the two bonds—those of Phelps and of the new issuer—of equivalent value.

In summary, when prevailing interest rates increase, the trading prices of previously issued bonds decrease. And when prevailing interest rates decrease, the trading prices of previously issued bonds increase.

Note, then, that when you trade in bonds, you will receive the interest payments specified in the bond agreement (called an indenture) at the time it was originally issued, and you will also be subject to possible gains or losses in the market prices of bonds, as prevailing interest rates change. Furthermore, should the credit-worthiness of the issuing corporation or government entity decrease, you can expect that the market price of its outstanding bonds will decrease, and vice versa.

In financial media (e.g., the *Wall Street Journal*) the listings for bond markets show for each bond issue the name of the borrower, the coupon rate, the maturity date (these three do not change), and then the current price and current yield to maturity—these last two reflect the effects of trading in the bonds.

In summary, an investor in a bond, corporate or governmental, will receive the coupon rate of interest so long as he or she owns it, but may also experience capital gains or losses on his or her investment as the market prices of the bond adjust to reflect changes in prevailing interest rates.

For example, in mid-2012, prevailing interest rates were at nearly a historic low. Therefore, one can anticipate that outstanding high-quality bonds were selling at a premium. If fact, in early July 2012, when this is being written, most bond prices showed just this effect, as illustrated in the table below. Generally, at the time bonds are just issued, their coupon rate is set very close to the prevailing interest rates, and thus the bonds initially sell at or near $100.

Issuer	Coupon%	Maturity	Rating	Price	Yield-to-Maturity%
Citigroup	4.5	Jan 2022	A-	$104.207	3.965
Goldman Sachs	6.75	Oct 2037	BBB+	$99.600	6.782
Caesars Casino	11.25	Jun 2017	B	$109.125	6.789
Wells Fargo	2.1	Jan 2017	A+	$100.813	1.923

Note from this table: (a) Goldman Sachs is the only bond selling below 100, and thus, its yield to maturity is slightly above its coupon rate. Because its maturity is twenty-five years out, the current very low prevailing short-term interest rates do not have much effect; (b) Citigroup, with maturity only twelve years out sells at over $100 to cause its yield to maturity to be below its coupon rate; (c) Caesars must have been issued as a junk bond since its coupon rate is 11.250, but now its yield to maturity is about the same as Goldman Sachs, with a much closer-in maturity date and a somewhat lower bond rating; (d) Wells Fargo has the highest rating and the shortest time to maturity (4.5 years); its yield to maturity and its coupon rate are not far apart, and therefore its price is at a very small premium. Notice also that this bank is borrowing at a much lower interest rate than its competitor, Citigroup.

Government Borrowing

Because the Treasury Department of the U.S. government is the dominant player in the bond market, its borrowing deserves a further word.

All federal government borrowing is unsecured. In effect, the government's taxing authority provides a form of assurance that the government will live up to its promises to repay its borrowings. Default on federal borrowing would be cataclysmic for this or any other issuing nation.

On almost an everyday basis, the Treasury borrows new funds and pays off debt as it matures. The federal government issues debt of widely varying maturities—from ninety days to about thirty years.

Short-maturity federal government borrowings are referred to as Treasury Notes and Treasury Bills (T-bills).

The Treasury from time to time issues bonds with unusual features that may appeal to various individual or institutional

Treasury Notes and Treasury Bills (T-bills): Represent intermediate-term and short-term borrowing by the federal government with relatively short maturities; some T-bills have maturities as short as ninety days.

Municipal Bonds: Bonds issued by cities and certain other organizations such as educations institutions; they are "tax free"; that is, interest payment on these bonds are not subject to Federal income tax to the recipients.

purchasers. For example, "zeros" (as they are called) provide for a zero coupon rate: no interest payments during the years the bonds are outstanding, but full payment of the face value at maturity. These bonds sell, of course, at a deep discount from their face value, the discount being equivalent to the interest that would have been paid on a normal bond. Treasury also sells what are called "TIPS," bonds that provide inflation-adjusted returns to the investors.

As mentioned earlier, governmental units in this country other than the federal government—primarily states and municipalities (cities)—borrow in the credit markets. Most of this borrowing is intermediate- to long-term, and like Federal Treasury borrowing, the credit instruments (bonds) are traded in the public markets (although their markets are somewhat less robust than the markets for Treasury securities.)

The U.S. Congress has long provided that interest that investors receive from municipal bonds is *not* subject to Federal income tax: that is, the recipients need not include these interest receipts in their taxable income. This provision permits these bonds to be sold at much lower coupon (interest) rates. Note that a bond investor in the 33 percent incremental income tax bracket will earn 4 percent (that is, 6 percent times 0.67) on a 6 percent "taxable bond", a corporate or federal government bond. This is the same after-tax interest rate as a 4 percent municipal bond coupon, because its interest payments are not taxable as income to the recipients.

Yield (Interest) Curves

We can generalize that borrowing for a long period of time (that is, with maturity dates ten or twenty years in the future) usually carries a higher interest rate (and thus generates a higher yield for the owner/lender) than shorter-term borrowing. Why is this so? Because, the lender (that is, the buyer of a bond) is typically comfortable assessing the issuer's future financial health and likely credit conditions for say, two to five years. However, the further out the loan's maturity date, the greater the risk to the lender (bond owner) that unforeseeable events may intervene to jeopardize ultimate repayment by the borrower or alter prevailing interest rates substantially.

Yield curves have "years to maturity" on the X-axis and interest rates on the Y-axis. A typical curve starts low on the Y-axis (but not zero, as even borrowing overnight has a cost) and is upward sloping, flattening considerably after say, five or eight years.

However, like all markets, the interest rate market is subject to the effects of demand and supply imbalances. When credit is scarce, with many individuals, corporations, and government units wanting to borrow, interest rates will increase. In 2008–2009, in the midst of a recession, credit was very available (partly because of actions taken by the federal government), demand for credit was light (there seemed to be very few attractive opportunities to invest funds that one might borrow), and interest rates were an almost unbelievable bargain! This condition persisted throughout 2012.

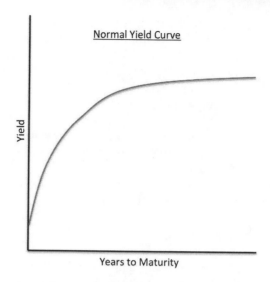

Expectations regarding inflation also strongly affect the interest rate curve. When inflation is high, lenders—who will now be repaid with inflated currency—demand high interest rates. The result may be a so-called inverted yield curve: short-term rates higher than long-term rates.

Complex Bonds

Over the last few decades the public credit markets have become very complex and complicated, with many new "products" being introduced by investment banks and others.

Three to four decades ago, the so-called junk bond was created: bonds with high yields (interest rates) and low credit ratings. As mentioned earlier, investors in these bonds trade high returns for a higher risk of default. Despite the name "junk," there is nothing sinister about these bonds. They are an important source of credit for companies with attractive investment opportunities but with balance sheets that won't support investment-grade ratings for its bonds.

Another innovation: "packaging" (aggregating) many small loans together such as home mortgages, credit card balances, and auto loans to permit them to be sold in the public market in very large dollar amounts. This financing passes the risk of default by the homeowner, credit card user, and auto buyer to the purchasers of these bonds (typically institutions, but sometimes individuals.) You may recall 2008 when house prices slumped and many mortgages went into default; the value of bonds secured by these mortgages slumped, raising havoc with the balance sheets of certain institutions, including many commercial banks. The unwise, overzealous use of this source of credit contributed to the financial bust of 2008 and beyond.

Default Swap:
The equivalent of insurance; the seller of the swap promises to compensate the buyer of the swap for losses incurred, should the bond go into default.

Interest Swaps:
agreements providing for an exchange of fixed-rate interest obligations for floating-rate interest obligations between two parties, and vice versa.

Investment Bank: assists corporations, other financial institutions and very wealthy individuals in arranging debt and equity financing and in effecting mergers, acquisitions, and other major financial transactions. The fees charged for these investment-banking services are often complex and quite high.

Companies like AIG have undertaken to insure the repayment of certain bonds, in return for an insurance premium paid by the borrower; such insurance is referred to as a default swap: AIG guarantees payment even if the borrower defaults; this insurance permits the borrower to obtain lower-cost credit. Various interest swap arrangements may be negotiated; for example, a fixed interest rate can be swapped for a floating rate, or vice versa. Discussion of still more sophisticated "products"—including borrowing in different currencies—is well beyond the scope of this book.

Investment Banks

At this conclusion of a discussion of the credit markets (and as we transition in the next chapter to a discussion of equity markets), this seems an appropriate time for a brief introduction to the investment bank. Investment banks are very active in both of these markets.

U.S. law has, for many years, drawn a clear distinction between commercial banking (accepting deposits and making loans) and investment banking (participating in a broad array of what might be called "deal making and financing," some of it quite imaginative and perhaps risky). The Glass-Steagall legislation, enacted in the 1930s, prohibited companies from participating in both. The reason: protection of the depositor, because investment banking was thought to expose the commercial banking customers, its depositors, to too much risk. This prohibition has been eliminated by Congress and now virtually all large commercial banks engage in investment banking activities and vice versa. Indeed, the financial turmoil of 2008–2009 saw a great number of mergers—some urged or forced by the federal regulators—of investment and commercial banks. Bank of America now owns Merrill Lynch, Chase Manhattan Bank and J. P. Morgan are now combined, and Goldman Sachs, for years the country's most prestigious and successful investment bank, now has a commercial banking arm; and so forth.

Review Questions for Chapter 6:

1. When prevailing interest rates increase what typically happens to prices of outstanding bonds? Why?
2. What are the primary differences between the functions of a commercial bank and those of an investment bank?

3. Under what economic conditions is the yield curve likely to be flat?
4. Why might a borrower whose loan carries a floating interest rate enter into an interest swap to obtain a fixed interest rate?
5. Some investors are attracted to invest in bonds having a maturity at the "knee" of the yield curve, and "ride" the yield curve as those bonds move closer to maturity. What does it mean to "ride the yield curve"?

Chapter Seven

EQUITIES AND EQUITY MARKETS

Cause and effect run from the economy to the stock market, never the reverse.

—John Kenneth Galbraith

To build and support their operations, corporations gather funds from both shareholders and lenders. That is, they (a) borrow directly from lending institutions (e.g., banks); (b) sell bonds (i.e., debt instruments); and (c) sell equity (common stock and related instruments). The previous chapter concerned itself with bonds and borrowing (credit and credit markets) and this chapter focuses on equity and equity markets.

The final chapter (chapter 9) looks at equity securities from the viewpoint of individual and institutional investors.

Chapter 5 noted that corporations are the dominant form of business organization in this country, but sole proprietorships and partnerships are also very important. Although they far out-number corporations in sheer number of entities, they account for only a small percentage of total business conducted. Sole proprietorships and partnerships can borrow from individuals, banks and other institutions, but rarely in the public markets. However, equity investments come only from the sole proprietor himself or herself and from the partners. Further discussion of the pros and cons of these three forms of organization – for example, taxation and owner liability – are beyond the scope of this book.

Equity: Securities of a corporation that represent ownership. Common stock (shares) is the dominant type of equity security.

Sole Proprietorship: A business organization that has only one owner, no outstanding common stock, and typically no board of directors.

Partnership: a business organization that has several (sometimes many) owners, not necessarily with equal ownership among the partners, and has no outstanding common stock. Many professional service organizations (e.g. lawyers and accountants) utilize the partnership form of organization.

Equity – Common Stock

Common Stock
(common share):
the equity security
representing
ownership in
a corporation,
which carries the
right to vote in
the election of
directors and to
render judgment
on various
corporate policies.

Fiduciary Duty:
One who has a
fiduciary duty
takes care of
financial and
related matters
for another.
Fiduciaries
have a high
legal standard
of care, and
must take their
duties seriously.
Directors have a
fiduciary duty to
the corporation's
shareholders.

Dividends:
Periodic cash
payments by the
corporation, at the
discretion of the
board of directors,
in equal amounts-
per-share to all
shareholders.

All corporations have issued and sold shares of common stock to one or more shareholders. (Note: a single shareholder may own all the shares of a corporation, or they can be sold broadly to as many as millions of shareholders.) Some shareholders may be other corporations, including various kinds of financial institutions.

The term "share" is appropriate: it represents a share of the legal ownership of the corporation. When the corporation issues and sells the share, it promises the buying shareholder to invest the proceeds and operate the corporation for the benefit of all its shareholders.

The board of directors (sometimes called a board of trustees) governs the corporation and consists of a group of men and women who have a fiduciary duty (that is, a legal responsibility) to see that the interests of the owners of the corporation (share-holders) are fairly pursued. Some corporations have a "majority owner": an individual or a group acting together (e.g., a family), or another corporation, or a financial institution. Most very large corporations however may have no single shareholder who owns as much as 1 or 2 percent of the outstanding shares.

Shareholders expect returns on their common stock invest-ments. These returns come in two forms: dividends and in-creases in the market value (i.e., selling price) of the shares. Of course, market values can also decline. Should the corporation become bankrupt (see chapter 2), the share value may go to zero. However, shareholders are protected from further liability: that is, creditors of the bankrupt corporation cannot hold the shareholders accountable for repayment of the corporation's debts. (Note: laws do not provide sole proprietors and partners with similar protection.)

Dividends are "declared" by the board of directors from time to time. Some corporations pay dividends quarterly (i.e., ev-ery three months), some annually, some periodically but at no regular interval, and some pay no dividends at all. Note that at the time shares are issued and sold, the corporation makes no promise as to if, when, or how much the shareholder should expect in the way of dividend payments. This absence of a prom-ised return is the key difference between a share of stock and a bond and, accordingly, is the reason why selling bonds is a riskier way for a corporation to raise capital than selling common stock.

Why would a corporation pay no dividends? The short answers are these: (a) the board of directors feels that the corporation, in light of its other obligations, does not have sufficient cash to do so, and/or (b) the board feels that the corporation's investment opportunities (e.g., new products, new markets, acquisitions) are so attractive that the corporation should retain and reinvest—for the benefit of shareholders—the funds that would otherwise be paid out in the form of dividends.

For example, the very large and successful firm, Berkshire Hathaway, has not paid, and, according to its chief executive's announcements, does not plan to pay dividends. Instead, its management uses available cash to make other investments, often acquiring other companies. Berkshire-Hathaway's management apparently believes that shareholders, should they need or wish for periodic cash returns, should simply sell the appropriate number of shares of stock.

If enough shareholders dislike the dividend policy adopted by a board, they can gather together and vote in a new board of directors to effect a change in the policy.

To repeat: returns on investments in common stock are manifested in two forms: dividends and market price appreciation. For the past forty-five years, dividends paid to shareholders accounted for 42 percent of the total return and market price appreciation for 58 percent. Yet by another historic measurement, managements seem to be deemphasizing the payment of dividends; for the period of 1948 through 1993 companies in the Standard and Poor's 500 listing paid average dividends-per-share equal to about one-half of their average earnings-per-share (a payout of 50 percent of earnings). For the past twenty years, the payout of dividends has declined to an average of about 27 percent of earnings.

Trading Common Stocks

Once issued and sold to shareholders, shares of common stock trade among investors (subject to many restrictions imposed by federal, state, and other regulatory agencies; more about them later in this chapter.) This buying and selling among shareholders does not involve the corporation. The company's financial position and financial statements are not affected. The corporation does not set the price at which shares trade. Shares trade among owners of common shares at prices agreed upon by buyer and seller.

Thus it follows that the market price of the corporation's common stock bears no necessary relationship to the corporation's net worth. The so-called book value per share is simply the total net worth of the corporation divided by the number of shares of stock outstanding. Market value per share may be greater or less than the book value

Book-value-per-
share: The net
worth (taken from
the corporation's
balance sheet)
divided by
the number of
common shares
outstanding.

per share, as determined by the interaction of demand for and supply of shares among buyers and sellers.

In short, when prospective buyer A is optimistic about the future of company X and shareholder B is pessimistic, A and B should be able to negotiate a price at which A will buy B's shares and they will both feel satisfied.

Put another way, when among the shareholders of a company, there are many more optimistic buyers (A's) than pessimistic ones (B's), the market price per share will increase; and vice versa. If the number of shares offered for sale by investors in company X is greater than the aggregate demand for company X's shares by potential investors, the price-per-share of company X's stock will decline until supply and demand are approximately equal and the "market clears" (as economists say). The jargon of the financial world would say that more people are "bearish" (pessimistic) than "bullish" (optimistic) about company X.

Considering the stock market as a whole, when the prevailing view of investors is pessimistic, we are in a bear market; prices are on the decline.

Bear Market:
Occurs when
pessimism about
the economic
future drives stock
prices lower. The
reverse is called
a bull market.

Some share price movements appear to be rational and others irrational. So be it. Differences of opinion among investors (and their advisors) about a whole host of matters (some having to do with company X, others to do with the U.S. or world economic expectations, still others relating to politics) are what drive market prices.

Company managers are not indifferent to the price of their company's shares. Shareholders tend to be unhappy when the share price declines, and managements are likely to hear from unhappy shareholders! Moreover, senior officers of the corporation almost surely own company shares personally. Some managements carefully track and worry about their companies' share prices. These managements tend to spend a large amount of time keeping financial analysts on Wall Street informed about and "sold" on the bright future for their corporations. Other managements believe these activities are largely a waste of time.

Comparing Equity Market Prices

Suppose a share of Company P sells for $71 and a share of Company T sells for $38. Are P's shares more expensive than T's? Yes and no. Yes, on a per-share basis they are more expensive. But which of the two is a better value? One cannot tell without knowing more.

Suppose Company P for one reason or another would like to have the "price" of its shares lowered without changing the "value" of each share. Company P could then simply issue one additional share for each share outstanding and distribute these shares—one for one—free of charge to each shareholder. Each shareholder would then own twice as many shares, but his or her percentage ownership in the company would not change at all. And in a wholly rational world (if there is such a thing), P's share price would drop in half, to $35.50, and now P's shares would appear "less expensive" than T's.

This maneuver is called a two-for-one <u>stock split</u> or a 100 percent stock <u>dividend</u>, and is undertaken periodically by corporations for reasons that we don't need to consider just now. Some companies declare from time to time smaller stock dividends (say, 10 percent) often when they want to conserve corporate cash and thus are reluctant to increase cash dividends. Some shareholders and investment analysts view such declarations as positive signals from the company's management. And signaling can be important in influencing stock prices. However, note that this paper-shuffling exercise has no real economic consequence. If a particular shareholder owned 2.678 percent of the outstanding shares of this company before the stock dividend or stock split, he or she owns exactly the same percentage thereafter.

Stock Split: Declared by the board of directors, a stock split results in the shareholders each receiving one additional share—a two-for-one split—for each share owned. Splits can involve distribution of three-for-one and other ratios.

Stock Dividend: Similar to a stock split, except that the distribution to the shareholders is a fraction of a new share for each share owned.

Price/Earnings Ratios

There must be other ways, then, to compare the prices of P's and T's shares. The most common is what is called the <u>price/earnings, or P/E, ratio</u>: the ratio of the price-per-share to the earnings-per-share, or "eps"—the annual net income of the corporation divided by the total number of common shares outstanding among all shareholders.

Price/Earnings (P/E) Ratio: ratio of the price-per-common-share of a company divided by the corporation's earnings-per-share.

Now suppose the P/E ratio of P's shares is 14 (the price is 14 times the annual earnings-per-share) while T's P/E ratio is 11.

Now we can fairly say that investors are willing to pay more for P's shares than for T's. Shareholders must be more optimistic about the future of P Corporation than that of T.

Thus, while the P/E ratio is the best way to compare the relative prices of two stocks, it does not tell you what shares to buy and what shares to sell. Just as the price doesn't tell you whether to buy the $400 suit or the $700 suit, or the $7-per-pound brie cheese or the $3-per-pound cheddar cheese; the process by which investors decide to buy or sell shares in a particular company is much more complicated than a simple comparison of P/E ratios.

Yield

Yield: The annualized dividend-per-share divided by the price-per-share.

Return to the consideration of dividends for a moment. Another important stock market metric is the <u>yield</u> on a share of stock: the annualized <u>dividend-per-share</u> divided by the market price per share. The yield on a non-dividend-paying stock is, of course, zero. A high-yielding stock may appear to be a better value than a low-yielding stock, but hold on! First, the board of directors has complete discretion to reduce the amount of the dividend if and when it thinks appropriate. Second, if a non-dividend-paying corporation has many attractive investment opportunities that are expected to boost its future earnings—which would be reflected in a higher market price per share—the zero-yield stock may be the better investment.

Dividend-Per-Share: Total dollars paid out in dividends for the year divided by the number of shares outstanding.

As we will see again in the final chapter, there is no single magic number to tell you how to invest in the stock market.

Total Market Capitalization

What is a corporation "worth"? The logical answer is "What someone is willing to pay for it." Entire corporations are frequently bought and sold. Sometimes the payment is in cash and other times in newly issued shares of the acquiring corporation, with the share payment going to the shareholders of the acquired company.

Total Market Capitalization: A corporation's current mark price per share times the number of shares outstanding.

Another measure of the worth of a corporation is what is commonly referred to as its <u>total market capitalization</u>: the number of shares outstanding times the stock's current market price per share. To repeat, total market capitalization bears no necessary relationship to the "book" net worth of the corporation.

Moreover, an acquiring corporation cannot necessarily purchase a company for its total market capitalization. The actions of the buyer are likely to drive up the stock's market price and thus the company's total market capitalization.

Selling Newly Issued Common Stock

Corporations whose shares are not publicly traded may, from time to time, decide to sell additional shares of common stock in order to realize funds to invest in their operations. If the corporation is relatively small and (a) its current number of shareholders is limited, (b) the amount to be raised is modest, and (c) the relatively few new shareholders to be added are all sophisticated investors, the corporation is not legally restricted from simply proceeding without great fanfare with the transactions.

Who qualifies as a "sophisticated" investor? Generally, a person with substantial net worth and investing experience and/or with net income per year in excess of say, $200,000, will be considered "sophisticated." Why this test? In general, federal and state regulations of the sale and trading of equity securities are aimed at protecting the "unsophisticated" investor—often referred to, somewhat unkindly, as "widows and orphans" (despite the fact that some widows are very savvy about equity securities!). People deemed "sophisticated" are thought to be able to look out for themselves and need no special help or protection from government. The so-called unsophisticated investor relies on the SEC.

The Role of the Securities and Exchange Commission (SEC)

The primary securities regulator is the Federal Securities and Exchange Commission (the SEC) created in the 1930s during the Great Depression. Note its name: securities *and* exchange—it regulates both, but here we will focus only on securities regulations.

To put it simply, the role of the SEC is to ensure that investors have sufficient, truthful information to make well-informed investment decisions. Note the double test: sufficient or, in the parlance of regulators, full disclosure; truthful, accurate, and not misleading. Failure to meet this test exposes the company

> **Sophisticated Investors:** Individuals who, by virtue of high personal net worth and/or high current income are considered by the regulators of securities to be sophisticated and therefore in less need of regulatory protection.

> **Securities and Exchange Commission (SEC):** The Federal regulatory body that is charged with regulating the trading exchanges, the issuance of new shares by a corporation, and the periodic public reporting of financial and other key information by every corporation whose common shares are traded in the public markets.

Full Disclosure:
Occurs when the disclosing party (the corporation) has provided all information that would be relevant to a potential buyer or seller of shares in making his or her decision.

Class Action Suit: A legal proceeding brought by a group of individuals (the class) who believe the named defendant has damaged them.

Going Public: Refers to the time when the corporation first sells it shares of common stock broadly to the public.

Initial Public Offering (IPO): The method by which a corporation goes public.

to liability, with the possibility of being sued by investors (typically acting together as a group in what is called a class action suit) for damages. Investors will argue that they were "damaged" if soon after the transaction the market price of the shares drops sharply and further, that had the company's disclosures been more thorough and/or accurate, the investors would not have made the investments.

Don't underestimate how difficult this double test is to meet. For example, the corporation does not want to—and is not required to—disclose confidential information that would be harmful to its competitive position or would reveal inappropriate personal information about its managers or directors.

Note particularly that the SEC does not render judgment on whether the company's stock represents an attractive or unattractive investment opportunity. The SEC leaves that judgment to the potential buyer or seller of the stock and seeks only to be certain that the buyer or seller has all relevant information when making that judgment.

To minimize the possibility of a suit, a company's lawyers typically advise a very extensive disclosure in quite legalistic terms. The result may be such a lengthy disclosure—in legalistic terms with many qualifications—that investors are dissuaded from a careful reading of the disclosures. Thus, an overemphasis on disclosure can defeat its purpose.

Initial Public Offerings: IPOs

The SEC plays a particularly significant role at the time a corporation goes public, that is, has an initial public offering (IPO): first offers to sell shares to the broad general public, and not simply to a few handpicked sophisticated investors, as mentioned above. The SEC insists that potential investors be provided a prospectus, a booklet that has been thoroughly reviewed and approved in advance by the SEC, setting forth current and historical financial statements, a thorough discussion of the nature and any unusual features of the company's business operations, brief biographies of senior officers and directors, and a list of so-called risk factors that may negatively impact the company's future operations and financial results. This prospectus is required to be in the hands of the investor before his or her purchase is finalized. Remember that the SEC renders no opinion on whether the investment opportunity is favorable or unfavorable.

Once a company's shares are traded in organized markets, the company is required to file with the SEC annual and quarterly financial results and the accompanying narrative. It also must make timely reports of various other events such as changes in key officers, offers to acquire other companies or to be acquired, and so forth. All of these reports are readily available to all who may be interested through the SEC's website.

Subsequent Equity Financings

Once the stock of a company is publicly traded—that is, once it has "gone public"—the corporation may, from time to time, seek to raise substantial amounts of additional equity capital to help fund its expansion and growth. Once again, a prospectus is prepared and reviewed by the SEC.

The Underwriter's Role

Most IPOs and subsequent broad stock offerings are underwritten by investment banks—often referred to as "Wall Street firms" even if they are not located on New York City's Wall Street!

The key function of the underwriters (typically there is one or a few lead underwriters and many secondary, participating underwriters, who together form what is referred to as a syndicate) is to purchase the shares from the issuing corporation and then to sell, as quickly as possible, these shares to individual or institutional investors. Thus, their task is to market and distribute the shares to a large number of investors, so that after the offering, robust trading in the stock is facilitated. The underwriters' compensation is the difference between the offering price and the purchase price paid to the company by the underwriters. The underwriters take the risk that they will not be able to sell all the shares at the offering price. The price is typically finalized the night before the offering becomes effective; if the company's shares are already publicly traded, the price will typically be a small discount off the closing (last) market price on the day before the offering is effective. Then the final prospectus is printed overnight and the next morning the sales of shares are executed.

Prospectus: A detailed, printed legal document disclosing all facts, history, and risks relevant to the potential investor in newly issued common stock, provided to the potential investor before the purchase is finalized. These documents are thoroughly scrutinized by the SEC.

Underwritten: Refers to the process by which investment banks (the underwriters) purchase newly-issued securities from the corporation and then sell the securities to individual or institutional investors.

Offering Price: The price of the security offered to public investors at the time of a public offering.

The lead underwriters are deeply involved in the preparation of the offering prospectus, since they, like the issuing corporation, have the legal risk that the disclosures in the prospectus are not thorough and accurate. You can be certain that lawyers and financial auditors (independent third parties) for the issuing corporation, as well as the underwriters' lawyers, also play significant—and expensive—roles.

In the case of an IPO, underwriters negotiate the offering price with the issuing corporation. Remember that in advance of the IPO, the shares have no established market price. The underwriters must set the offering price high enough to gain agreement from the offering company and yet low enough to be attractive to potential buyers of the stock, who are typically customers of the underwriting firms' brokerage operations. This negotiation can be emotional and stressful.

Conventional wisdom is that both the issuing corporation and the underwriters would like the shares offered in an IPO to trade immediately or within a few days after the offering at a price at least 5 to 10 percent above the offering price. If the price jumps too much, the issuing corporation may feel that the offering price was unfairly low, and if the trading price falls below the offering price, not only will the initial buyers be unhappy but also the underwriters are likely to lose money, as they struggle to sell all of the shares in the offering.

Insiders: Directors, senior officers, certain other employees and early investors who almost surely have privileged information that is not available to the general investing public.

An argument for going public is to provide the corporation's existing shareholders—particularly insiders such as directors, senior officers, other employees and very early investors—with liquidity, i.e., the opportunity to sell shares they acquired while the company was private. Company employees may be particularly anxious to sell some of their shares in order to diversify their investments and thereby reduce investment risk (discussed more thoroughly in the final chapter.)

Private vs. Public Corporations

Liquidity: In this context, it refers to the ability of early shareholders to liquidate— realize on their investment by selling—some or all of the shares they own.

Once a corporation is public—that is, once its shares are actively traded—the corporation takes on the many and expensive duties of (a) issuing periodic financial and other reports to the SEC and its shareholders; and (b) meeting with security analysts and others to "tell the company's story." The purpose of this activity is to encourage purchase of the stock to maintain or enhance its market price. Moreover, the public company will almost inevitably become increasingly concerned that its quarterly earnings meet (or exceed) the expectations of the security analysts and its large shareholders, in order that its share market price does not plummet.

Many argue that this preoccupation with stock price and quarterly earnings—short-term thinking, if you will—may inhibit the corporation from making strategic, long-term decisions and investments that would be beneficial for the corporation, particularly if such decisions negatively impact near-term quarterly earnings.

Being public subjects the corporation to close scrutiny by present and potential investors and by the financial media. Some argue that this close scrutiny provides good discipline for corporate managers. Others claim it provides a distraction to management, time that might better be devoted to assuring the long-term success of the corporation.

This latter group tends to prefer that the corporations in which they are involved "remain private." Of course, remaining private is only an option if the corporation can obtain sufficient equity capital from sources other than the general public. This may be the case if the company is and remains small, and thus has no need for periodic major infusions of equity capital. Companies that remain private often provide an opportunity or, in some cases, a requirement that employee-shareholders who need to or want to sell some or all of their shareholdings, or those who leave the company, sell their shares back to the corporation. The price for such inside transactions is often set by formula related to recent earnings and/or to corporate net worth; and the corporation must have sufficient cash available to afford the purchases.

Repurchase of Outstanding Common Stock

In recent decades many public corporations have, from time to time, repurchased their shares. That is, the corporation becomes a buyer in the public market, bidding for its own shares.

Why would a corporation wish to buy, say, 10 percent of its outstanding shares? The reasons are generally a combination of the following:

1. The corporation has excess cash (or can borrow on very favorable terms) and feels that its share's current market price is low. (Caution: many managers, being enthusiastic about their companies' prospects, think the market is not "fairly" pricing their corporation's stock, and thus, the share price is a bargain.)
2. As the corporation effects these repurchases, it is "adding demand" to the market. Increased demand with no change in supply should increase the share's market price.
3. Once purchased, the shares are, in effect, retired and the number of outstand-

ing shares is reduced. The reduction in outstanding shares has the effect of increasing earnings-per-share by simply reducing the denominator of that ratio (that is, reducing the number of shares outstanding.) In turn, that increase will raise the share market price if the price/earnings ratio remains unchanged.

4. Sometimes the corporation is eager to repurchase the shares of one or a few large, dissatisfied (often called dissident) shareholders who are vocal and troublesome in expressing their dissatisfaction.

5. The reduction in shares—and thus net worth—has the effect of increasing debt leverage. And if the corporation borrows the funds to pay for the repurchases, the transactions have a double impact on the key debt-leverage ratio: increasing the numerator (debt) and decreasing the denominator (equity).

6. A corporation that announces its intentions to repurchase its own shares in the market place is sending a "signal" to its present and potential shareholders that management (and the Board) feels that the current market price is inappropriately low—that is, the current market price appears to be a "good buy."

However, in the past decade or so, many companies that repurchased shares soon thereafter found that their shares traded at a substantially lower price than the repurchase price. That is, the repurchase of shares proved not to be a "good buy."

Stock Exchanges: Physical and Electronic

Purchases and sales of outstanding equity shares are typically transacted on one of the many recognized stock exchanges. Let's start by considering the oldest, largest, and decreasingly important exchange in this country: the New York Stock Exchange (NYSE).

Corporations that wish to, and that meet the requirements of the New York Stock Exchange and pay a fee, may list their shares on the exchange. Brokers representing buyers and other brokers representing sellers make known to so-called specialists at the NYSE their clients' interest in buying or selling. The specialist negotiates with the buying and the selling brokers (or their representatives) to arrive at a price.

The NYSE has a physical location in lower Manhattan, New

Stock Exchanges (stock markets): Physical and/or electronic venues for trading securities of various kinds.

New York Stock Exchange, NYSE: The largest U.S. equity and bond trading market with a physical presence

List: Listing on a trading exchange requires the company register its shares and meet certain requirements demanded by the exchange managers.

York City, where these specialists are physically located. In these days of instant electronic communication, this sounds rather quaint—and it is. Increasingly today, buy/sell transactions are done electronically and in a fraction of a second.

A second important U.S. exchange, an electronic one with no physical presence, is <u>NASDAQ</u>, sometimes called the <u>over-the-counter market</u> and long ago called the "curb market" because the transactions were actually undertaken on the curb in front of the NYSE building!

> **NASDAQ (over-the-counter):** A large electronic market in this country tending to specialize in the trading of shares of newer and smaller companies. Its initials stand for National Association of Securities Dealers Automatic Quotation.

Generally speaking, the shares of smaller public companies trade on NASDAQ and those of larger companies trade on the NYSE.

Virtually all countries around the world—both industrialized and "emerging"—now have markets generally similar to those in the U.S. and specializing in the trading of stocks of corporations resident in their countries. Those in such cities as London, Paris, Frankfurt, Hong Kong, and Tokyo are analogous to the NYSE.

The final chapter has more to say about these markets from the viewpoint of the investor.

The Venture Capital Market

Some informal markets are also important as sources of equity capital for corporations. One that is widely reported on is the so-called <u>venture capital (VC)</u> market.

> **Venture Capital:** Consists of pools of capital entrusted by wealthy individuals and institutions to partnerships that in turn invest the funds in small, young, and potentially rapidly growing corporations.

Venture capital firms provide start-up and early-stage companies with capital, typically in the form of equity (or equity related), to found and/or grow their businesses. This market was essentially nonexistent before World War II but grew significantly during the last three decades of the twentieth century and has continued to expand in this century. The United States led the world in creating and refining this market, primarily because entrepreneurial effort and success has flourished in this country like nowhere else. But the rest of the developed and developing worlds are running hard to catch up.

The hotbeds of venture capital investing have been the San Francisco peninsula (the iconic Silicon Valley) and Boston.

Some contend that the impetus for this development came from strong universities: Stanford and UC–Berkeley in the Silicon Valley area, MIT and Harvard in Boston. Endless other countries have attempted to emulate the success of Silicon Valley, often with their governments trying to assist.

Venture capital companies are generally formed as limited partnerships. The task of finding and nurturing start-up and young companies is that of the general partners, who invest some money, but typically not a large percentage of the partnership's total funds. The funds come dominantly from so-called limited partners: very wealthy individuals, endowments of educational or philanthropic enterprises, pension funds, insurance firms, and others. These investors typically have (a) a high tolerance for risk: equity investments in start-up and young companies are unquestionably risky; and (b) an eagerness for very high returns, which is the goal of all venture capital firms.

New firms face a high risk of failure. Of course, those risks are mitigated if the entrepreneurial teams, as well as the VC general partners making the decision to invest, are both experienced and capable.

VCs look for the potential of very high returns—say, ten times their investment in five years, which calculates out (see chapter three) to an annual return of about 35 percent compounded, a very handsome return indeed. If out of, say, 10 investments, two or three earn such high (or even higher) returns, four earn far more modest returns, and four fail, losing all the invested capital, the VC firm overall may still be quite successful. To use a baseball analogy, if the VC partnership hits two home runs and four singles, while striking out four times, over the course of 10 at bats, its RBI (runs batted in) will probably be darn good! Its limited partners will be quite happy and the general partners will become quite wealthy.

Carried Interest: The percentage of the total capital gains earned by a private venture capital fund that accrues to the fund's general partners as compensation for their management efforts.

The general partners earn their compensation in two forms. Typically, they receive an annual fee equivalent to about 2 percent of the capital invested in the partnership. In addition, they will have what is called a carried interest in the partnership entitling them to say, 20 percent of the total returns for no capital investment.

At start-up, the entrepreneurial team is provided stock ownership in their company substantially greater than the team's personal investments. Then as their company develops, they will be granted additional equity ownership (in one form or another). The VCs want the entrepreneurial team to have a significant equity interest to assure that the team has high incentive to cause the new company to succeed.

The payoff opportunity for the entrepreneurial team and the VC investors typically comes when either (a) a much larger company acquires the start-up or young company, or (b) the young company goes public and the investors begin selling their shares into the public market. Generally, there is no expectation that the company will ever repay—directly or indirectly—to the VC firm the capital the partnership invested.

As you likely know, some of these payoffs have been truly spectacular. As has been true for at least a century and a half, successful entrepreneurs have become some of the country's largest and most generous philanthropists. While many people object to the very high salaries and bonuses paid to top managers in some large firms, few people resent or begrudge handsome entrepreneurial payoffs. They are the returns for innovating, creating new products and markets, taking major career and financial risks, working very hard for an extended period, and doing all this in an ethical manner (typically) under the close oversight of the VC partners.

Frequently, VC partnerships specialize in one or more ways: perhaps by geographic region; perhaps by type of business (e.g., biotech, electronic, software, internet); perhaps by stage of company development (e.g., start-up capital, second-round investing when risk of failure has diminished somewhat, or third-round investing when risk has diminished further.)

Some operating (i.e., nonfinancial) corporations have entered the VC business. Examples are pharmaceutical and technology companies. Typically, these companies are motivated both by high potential returns and by the opportunities to have early and close-up looks at new innovations and developing markets, sometimes with the hope or expectation that they may be able to acquire some of the companies in which they invest.

Postscript: Preferred Stock; Convertible Stocks and Bonds

This chapter has focused on "common" stocks. You should be aware, however, of another form of stock (although it is used infrequently): <u>preferred stock</u>. "Preferreds," as they are often called, have some features akin to a bond and others akin to common stock. Like a bond they have a face value and a stated return rate (called "dividend" rather than "interest"). Like a stock, the preferred has no maturity date and the issuing corporation is not obligated to redeem the preferred nor even to pay the dividend—at least not to pay it on time. Preferreds occupy an interesting financing niche; a discussion of their somewhat unique uses is a bit beyond the scope of this book.

Importantly, most preferreds—and some bonds—are convertible into common stock.

<u>Preferred Stock:</u>
A seldom used security that has some characteristics of bonds and some characteristics of common stocks. They are often convertible into common stock at a pre-agreed ratio.

<u>Convertible securities:</u>
Securities that may in the future be exchanged under certain prearranged conditions for common stock. They are most often either bonds or preferred stock.

That is, the owner of convertible preferred stock or convertible bonds has the option of exchanging them for a preset number of common shares. For example, an offering of $100 bonds, sold when the issuing corporation's common stock was selling for $35 per share, might include a conversion rate of two common shares per bond. The buyer of the bond enjoys the low risk associated with a fixed-income security but also has the opportunity to share in future common stock price appreciation if the company turns out to be very successful. The convertible bond owner would surely not convert until the common stock price is well above $50 per share.

Review Questions for Chapter 7:

1. What are the primary reasons that a corporation might decide to repurchase some of its outstanding shares?

2. Assuming a private corporation does not have a pressing need in its business for additional capital, why might it, nevertheless, decide to have an initial public offering (IPO)?

3. Why are corporate directors considered to be fiduciaries?

4. If a share of a particular public company has a P/E of 11 and a market price of $37 per share, what are its earnings-per-share?

5. What is the yield on the common stock of a corporation that pays no dividends?

6. What is meant by "full disclosure"? Is full disclosure an unreasonable standard to which the SEC holds public corporations?

7. How is the selling price per share established for an initial public offering (IPO)?

8. What financial risks are the underwriting financial institution exposed to when it conducts an initial public offering for a client corporation?

9. What operating advantages do private companies have over public companies? What disadvantages?

10. Should an investor in Clark Corporation be pleased or disappointed when Clark announces a plan to repurchase (in the market) some of its outstanding common shares? Why?

Chapter Eight

OTHER INVESTMENT MARKETS

Never invest your money in anything that eats or needs repairing.

—Billy Rose

Gambling: a principle inherent in human nature.
—Edmund Burke

Chapters 6 and 7 reviewed the credit and equity markets, respectively. Most individuals look to these markets for opportunities to invest funds for retirement, for bequests to children, to accomplish philanthropic plans, and to achieve other long-term financial goals. The wealthy and more adventuresome among us may seek less traditional vehicles for deploying funds. This chapter introduces some of those vehicles.

One caveat at the outset: no bright line differentiates investment opportunities from speculative (gambling) opportunities. And speculation is neither illegal nor immoral; it is simply not an appropriate subject for this book.

> Speculation: Speculating in the financial markets is gambling, not investing.

The general flow of this chapter is from those opportunities that are reasonable alternatives to direct investing in stocks and bonds, to those that are probably best left to the seasoned professional or avoided altogether.

The best safety is in fear.

—William Shakespeare

Long/Short Investing

Most of us who purchase shares of Company X on the stock market do so primarily because we expect the market price of X's stock to increase. That is called <u>investing long.</u>

Suppose that you feel quite strongly that the outlook for another company, Company Y, is negative and therefore you anticipate that Y's share price will decline. How can you act on your conviction and benefit financially if in fact Y's share price falls? You can <u>sell</u> Y's shares <u>short</u>. Since you don't presently own Y shares, you will need to borrow them, paying a small fee for the privilege and promising to return the shares on a certain date in the future. You then sell these shares at today's price, anticipating that you can purchase the replacement shares before the return date at a price-per-share below today's price. Your gain (or loss): the difference between today's price and the replacement price, times the number of transacted shares, less the small borrowing fee.

Who lends shares so that short-sellers can participate in the market in this way? Primarily large institutions (e.g., endowment funds, bank trust departments, insurance companies, and mutual funds) that: (a) have major "long" positions in the companies whose shares they are willing to lend; (b) expect to be long-time investors in these companies (although they may increase or decrease their positions in the short term); (c) seek to improve their overall investment performance by gaining the modest "rent" paid by the borrower; and (d) believe that the lending contract involves little risk because they have confidence that the borrower (the counterparty) will perform on his or her end of the lending agreement. Investment banks that match potential "borrowers" and "lenders" earn modest commissions from this matchmaking.

Note that the potential loss from short selling is greater than the potential loss from long investing, since the price of a share that you own "long" cannot go below zero, while there is no upper limit to the possible price gain on a share that you are "short."

Does short selling add to or mitigate price <u>volatility</u> in the market? Experts disagree on that question. Unquestionably, short selling can manipulate the market in ways that can be harmful to the company whose shares are involved. From time to time, the Securities and Exchange Commission considers placing various restrictions on short-selling, but the practice is unlikely to be outlawed entirely, in part because no agreement prevails as to whether volatility is a net positive or negative for the stock markets.

The aggregate number of shares of a particular stock that have been sold short is relevant to future movements of its price. At some point, all of those short positions must be "covered" (the shares bought back in the open market and returned to the lenders) and those future purchases represent latent demand for the stock; the purchase of replacement shares will tend to boost the market price per share.

Put and Call Options

Another way to participate in the market is to write options. A put option gives the owner the right (but not the obligation) to sell a given number of shares at a specified price on or before a given date. A broker helps the writer find the counterparty for such a transaction: that is, the individual or institution that will pay the writer if he or she exercises the put option. Of course, the writer of the put pays a fee to the counterparty for this right (and some smaller fee to the broker.) An investor worried about sharp price declines in the market price of a particular stock he or she owns might write a put option for protection on the downside.

A call option is the opposite: the writer acquires the right to buy a given number of shares at a specified price higher than the current market price by a given date. Call options permit the writers to participate in a share-price increase without owning the shares outright. If the share price never rises to the call price, the writer simply lets the option lapse.

Warning: trading in puts and calls resembles speculation (or gambling) more than investing.

Rapid ("Day") Trading

Some Wall Street firms engage in rapid trading (buying and selling) of securities, typically in large dollar amounts, seeking to capture small advances in share prices or avoid small declines. Some individuals seek to emulate these practices (generally in small dollar amounts); they are typically referred to as day trad-

Writing Options: refers to entering into a contract with a counterparty that provides the writer the right (but not requirement) to effect a transaction with the counterparty within a specified period of time.

Put Option: gives the writer the opportunity (but not obligation) to sell an agreed upon number of specified shares at a specified price on or before the option's termination date.

Call Option: gives the writer the opportunity (but not obligation) to buy an agreed upon number of specified shares at a specified price on or before the option's termination date.

ers. This practice has been made possible by the sharp decline over the last several decades in stock-trading transaction costs. Fair to say that this practice, too, is better labeled as "speculation" than investing, and left to the full-time professionals.

Mutual Funds

Mutual funds are very widely viewed as an alternative to investors choosing and owning individual stocks. In simple terms, mutual funds pool monies from many investors and contract with professional money management organizations to manage the monies (for a fee); the money managers purchase securities (debt or equity) appropriate to the stated objective of the mutual fund. The largest mutual fund complexes in this country today are: Vanguard, Fidelity and American Funds; mutual fund management is the dominant business of each of these three companies. Mutual funds are also operated by some banks (e.g., Wells Fargo Bank, Bank of New York Mellon), some brokerage firms (e.g., Schwab, Merrill Lynch), and many, many smaller investment management companies. Mutual fund operations are highly regulated by the Securities and Exchange Commission.

The operators of mutual funds charge fees for their services; these annual fees tend to run between 0.3 percent (referred to as 30 basis points) and 2.0 percent (200 basis points) of the market value of the mutual fund share.

Mutual funds calculate and publish their NAV (net asset value per share) at the end of each day the securities markets are open and operating. NAV is equal to the total market value of all investments held by the mutual fund, divided by the number of mutual fund shares outstanding. The mutual fund investor may purchase or redeem ("cash in") shares at this NAV during the following day, at the end of which a new NAV is calculated.

Interestingly, today there are more mutual funds in this country than there are individual stocks that trade in the market. Mutual funds are owned by a high percentage of U.S. households. Some of these funds are very large—upward of $200 billion—and others are small and highly specialized. Fees charged by the investment managers vary quite widely, and, unsurprisingly, investment performance also varies quite widely among mutual funds and over time.

The stated objective of the fund is the key to helping the individual investor decide which fund, or set of funds, best matches his or her needs. Some mutual funds are so-called growth funds, concentrating their share ownership among companies with above-average growth prospects. Others are "balanced" funds, investing in both equity and debt securities. Still others specialize in investments in certain industries or certain countries or areas of the world. Some mutual funds focus on providing their shareholders with above-average income; they tend to invest in companies paying high dividends, as well as in debt securities. A firm that does quite a credible job of evaluating mutual fund performance is Morningstar.

The ability of an individual mutual fund to achieve excellent performance over time is subject to widespread debate. Here is a warning recently sounded by Daniel Kahneman, a highly regarded, Nobel prize-winning statistician: "Mutual funds are run by highly experienced and hardworking professionals who buy and sell stocks [and other investment securities] to achieve the best possible results for their clients. Nevertheless, fifty years of research is conclusive: at least two out of every three mutual funds underperform the market in any given year."

Money-Market Funds

A useful subset of mutual funds is the so-called money-market funds. These mutual funds invest in short-term, fixed-rate debt securities such as T-bills and commercial paper (which are saleable instantly, and seldom vary much in price). These funds are typically both bought and sold for—that is, have a constant NAV of—one dollar. Even during the turmoil of 2008–2009, most retained their one-dollar valuation. Many people use these funds, rather than bank savings accounts, to park short-term emergency funds and excess cash balances. They are low-risk, low-return investment vehicles.

"Load"/"No-Load" Funds

Mutual funds sold through the brokerage community are generally <u>load funds</u>: they charge a sales commission (averaging about 4 to 5 percent), most of which goes to the selling broker; a few charge small redemption fees as well. Other mutual funds are considered <u>no-load</u>: no sales agent is involved—investors can easily and quickly acquire or redeem shares via the Internet or by telephone—and thus, no commission is charged.

<u>Money-Market Funds:</u> Mutual funds that invest in short-term, fixed-rate debt securities and typically maintain an NAV of one dollar.

<u>"Load" Fund:</u> A mutual fund that charges the purchaser/investor an upfront sales commission, most of which goes to the selling broker.

<u>"No-load Funds":</u> These mutual funds are typically not sold through brokers and thus change no commission.

Why would you choose to invest in a load fund rather than a no-load fund? Because you need or value the guidance of the broker in formulating and executing your personal financial plan, including recommending specific mutual funds for you to invest in.

Remember that both load and no-load funds charge annual fees for investment management services and to cover miscellaneous expenses. These fees are generally not trivial and directly reduce the overall performance of the fund. Since, as Dr. Kahneman says, most funds are hard-pressed to "beat the averages" consistently, fee levels should be a major criterion when selecting among mutual funds.

Indices

Before describing index funds, we need to delve a bit deeper into the nature of stock market indices and their construction.

The indices most reported and quoted by the U.S. media are (a) the Dow Jones industrial average (DJI) comprised of thirty large industrial stocks excluding transportation, mining, retailing and many other sectors of the economy and the stock market; (b) the Standard and Poor's 500 (S&P 500) comprised of the 500 largest U.S. companies; and (c) the NASDAQ index that includes all stocks listed on the NASDAQ electronic market.

Any statistician will tell you that an index of 500 stocks is more reliable than one of thirty (and remember, those are limited to industrial companies.) My guess as to why the DJI dominates market reporting is that Dow Jones (the company that calculates the DJI) also publishes the *Wall Street Journal*, the daily newspaper of record for Wall Street; that paper has reason to emphasize its own index. (The S&P 500 is calculated by the Standard and Poor's Company, the same outfit that is one of the three rating agencies for bonds.)

In practice the DJI and S&P 500 indices track each other surprisingly closely. The calculation of each index is complicated both because the list of thirty and the list of 500 do not stay constant, and because the number of shares that a corporation has outstanding changes with stock splits, stock dividends, share-based acquisitions, and the sale of newly issued shares. Each of DJI and S&P has worked out an algorithm that removes the effect of such changes.

The indices are quoted in dollars. At the time of this writing, the DJI has a value of about $12,500 and the S&P 500 has a value of about $1,350. The fact that the DJI value is more than nine times the value of the S&P 500 is irrelevant. What investors and stock analysts care about are the changes in value, not the absolute value. Unfortunately, these changes are also described in dollar amounts; thus, on an average stock market day, the DJI will change by about nine times as many dollars as will the S&P 500. The better measure of index changes is in terms of percentages, not dollars. A major change in the indices might be a one-day movement of more than 2 percent.

Nearly an infinite number and variety of stock market indices exist; the other important ones focus on single industries and foreign stock exchanges.

Index Funds

Over the years some financial market theoreticians have asserted that the stock market is <u>efficient</u>: market prices are a full reflection of what is known about the company and its prospects. If the market is truly efficient, an individual investor—professional or amateur—seldom can "beat the market," that is, over a number of years consistently earn a return higher than the average return earned by all investors. Accordingly, they argue, the individual is best off just "buying the market." So-called <u>index funds</u> permit the investor to do just that!

For example, you could buy shares in an index fund that tracks (mimics the price movements of) the Standard and Poor's 500 index, the Dow Jones Industrial Average, or an index of the Hong Kong stock market, pharmaceutical companies, public utility companies, or those in other industries. To accomplish this tracking, the managers of index funds need not buy *all* the securities in the index, but rather just a sufficient sample. Over the short history of index funds, managers have succeeded in minimizing the <u>tracking error</u>: the difference between the performance of the fund and the performance of the corresponding index. As you might imagine, the fees charged by index funds (referred to as <u>passive investments)</u> are quite low—much lower than those of so-called <u>actively managed</u> funds—since very little research or expertise is required to construct and operate an index fund.

Commodities

Some brave, risk-tolerant individuals invest in what are called <u>commodities</u>. A commodity has full fungibility: that is, the market treats it as equivalent, or nearly so, no matter who supplies it. Examples are petroleum and copper (and also many agricultural products such as wheat, corn and soybeans). The price of copper, for example, is universal, and fluctuates daily based on global supply and demand.

Efficient: An efficient market is one where market prices fully reflect all that is known about the companies that issued the securities. Individual investors are unlikely to beat the average return of all investors in an efficient market.

Index Fund: A mutual fund with a performance objective of meeting, but not beating, the returns of a particular index—a market-wide index, a country index, an industry index, and so forth.

Tracking Error: The difference in investment performance between that of an index fund and that of the index that the fund tracks or mimics.

Passive investment: Funds for which security selection is predetermined by the index selected. Index funds are passively invested.

Manufacturers of packaged food products or electrical equipment are regular participants in the commodities markets with the aim of securing at advantageous prices materials that they will use in their manufacturing processes.

Individuals who buy and sell commodities, often called <u>trading in futures</u>, are simply betting on future movements in market prices. Thus, this activity too can be fairly characterized as speculation, not investing.

One can also buy and sell currency futures to speculate on changes in exchange rates among the currencies of different countries. Many companies with substantial international activities turn to these same currency futures markets to hedge—that is, offset or neutralize the currency risks associated with—the amounts of foreign currency they owe to foreign entities or foreign customers owe them.

A particularly interesting commodity is gold. Historically, of course, gold was used as a currency by many societies. Some individuals, particularly during uncertain economic times, continue to feel that gold is the ultimate secure investment, preferable to holding assets denominated in US dollars, the Euro, or other currencies. (Those attracted to investing in gold may also be attracted to Swiss francs, a currency that over the years has held its value while other currencies have been buffeted by inflation.) Remember, though, that, unlike interest earned on fixed-income securities, gold (and Swiss francs) provide no return during the years one holds them and, moreover, in the case of gold one must pay annually about one percent of its value for safe storage (assuming you are wiser than to store it in your basement or under your bed.) Accordingly, to buy gold is simply to speculate on its price; buying gold is a gamble, not an investment.

Limited-Partnership Pools of Private Capital

In recent decades, the business landscape, including the financial markets, has been much influenced—even reshaped—by private pools of capital. Some of the high-profile names of very large private capital pools are Bain, Carlyle, KKR, Blackstone, Soros, and Apollo. The source of the funds and the investment objectives of these pools of capital vary widely, but they tend to have the following common characteristics.

First, they are—indeed, they must be—funded by wealthy individuals or by institutions who don't need (or at least are presumed not to need) the protection of the Securities and Exchange Commission and other regulatory agencies. They are sophisticated investors with sufficient wealth that they can "afford to lose" their funds invested in these pools.

Many of these investors are institutions, not individuals. For example, large university endowments, philanthropic foundations, pension funds, and the like have committed substantial funds to such limited partnerships. Indeed, the handsome returns earned by the Harvard, Yale, and Stanford endowments, among others, are attributable to their early involvement in these high-risk, high-return investment vehicles.

Second, the structure of these funds is typically a limited-partnership. Those few individuals responsible for raising the funds and then making and managing the investments are the so-called general partners. The "silent partners" with no management responsibility (i.e., the investors) are limited partners.

> **General Partners:** The general partner(s) actively manage the partnership's business, are compensated differently than the limited partners, and bear some risk over and above that borne by the limited partners. All partnerships must have at least one general partner.

The fees charged to the limited partners are similar to those of VC partnerships (see chapter 7). The common annual fee structure—2 percent of the total asset value of the fund plus 20 percent of the increase in asset value—has resulted in stunning fortunes for some of the general partners, as well as solid returns for the limited partners. However, by no means are all these funds successful.

Despite their similarities, the diversity in the ways in which these pools are deployed is quite wide. Here are a few:

> **Limited (Silent) Partners:** Contribute funds to the partnership but do not have operational responsibility. Their participation must be limited in order for them to avoid some of the risks to which the general partners are exposed.

a. General private equity funds. These large aggregations of invested funds are used to take major equity positions in existing public or private companies, typically such large positions as to be able to influence the future strategies of the target companies. Sometimes these stock acquisitions are "friendly"—accomplished through negotiation with the company's present management—and sometimes they are "unfriendly." Unfriendly acquisitions of large equity positions are often referred to as raids, particularly when the private equity fund seeks to change the management team in hopes of achieving improved profit performance in the years ahead.

b. Leveraged-buyout (LBO) funds. The general partners of these funds search for companies that (a) appear to be underperforming, and thus, their stock prices are depressed, and (b) have either substantial cash on hand or balance sheets that would permit them to borrow substantial sums. Once the fund has acquired a significant position in the target company, its partners typically see to it that (a) struggling lines of business are sold or terminated, (b) underutilized assets (perhaps whole divisions) are sold, (c) expenses are sharply reduced, and (d) large sums of money are borrowed by the company to buy up some or all of its existing shares. Once these measures—sometimes draconian— are taken, and performance is improved, the LBO fund will exit the investment by selling or merging the company or once again taking it public.

Market Neutral:
Investing that seeks to make gains in both up-markets and down-markets. Short-selling, the use of puts and calls, and other high-risk, potentially high-return strategies are employed by the partners of these funds.

c. Hedge funds. The term "hedge" covers a myriad of strategies. A hedge fund is a private, actively managed investment fund using sophisticated, often mathematical, strategies (developed by the so-called rocket scientists of Wall Street!) in international and/or domestic markets designed to offset losses during a market downturn and/or generate returns higher than traditional stock and bond investments. Some hedge funds seek to be market neutral: able to achieve positive returns whether the market moves up or down. These funds make heavy use of short positions. Another strategy used is to accumulate a significant equity position in a company that the general partners believe will soon be acquired at a significant step-up in its current stock price. The range of strategies that might be employed is limited only by the ingenuity of the general partners (and their investment bankers) and their willingness to expose the fund to substantial risks.

Arbitrage:
Capitalizing on price differences among two or more markets.

d. Arbitrage funds. Arbitrage takes advantage of price differences among two or more markets, executing offsetting transactions—that is, buying in one market and selling in the other. The profit realized is the difference between the prices in the two markets. To make a meaningful profit when such price differences are very small requires that many large-dollar transactions be executed. Arbitrage opportunities were more prevalent when financial and market information moved more slowly. Now arbitragers must be prepared to act at lightning speed, often using very sophisticated securities and huge amounts of capital.

Real Estate Investing

Omitted from this book is much discussion of the <u>real estate market</u>. Please don't conclude from this omission that real estate investing is inappropriate for individuals. Indeed, for many of us, the biggest single investment we will ever make is in our homes, and that investment will be rolled forward into subsequent homes that we will purchase and occupy.

<u>Real Estate Market:</u> The venue for buying and selling real estate. The market is very diverse: geographically, by type of real estate, by size of transaction, and so forth.

For decades—from the Great Depression of the 1930s until about 2008—the conventional wisdom was that residential real estate prices increase continually, albeit at different annual rates, and they never suffer serious price declines. Unfortunately, certain government policies and lending practices reinforced this conventional wisdom and mortgage lenders bought into it. Furthermore, this led to some foolish decisions by individuals: buying a bigger, more expensive home than they could afford; buying a second and even a third home; and/or buying for rental purposes, a condominium or vacation home. In each of these cases, the assumption was that the future sale price of the real estate would be the overpowering factor in determining the return on the real estate investment.

This conventional wisdom exploded in 2008 and the subsequent four years during which prices continued to decline in many regions of the country, particularly where overbuilding had occurred and real estate speculation by individuals was rampant.

Still, over the sweep of history, investments in owner-occupied properties have been sound. For many of us, the "returns" come in both financial and psychic terms (that is, we enjoy owning the home in which we live.)

Will the above-mentioned conventional wisdom—or another— create another "bubble" in the years and decades ahead? Probably. We may hope that it will not lead to the foolish investing and lending that created the "real estate bubble" of recent years. But a caveat: the history of markets is that bubbles occur periodically and not just in real estate, and when they burst, individual investors are hurt.

Of course, without owning lands and buildings outright, one may invest indirectly in real estate by buying the securities of companies whose business is to (a) invest in real estate—typically commercial, industrial, or multifamily residential; (b) develop real estate projects; (c) build new commercial, industrial, or residential units; or (d) manage existing real estate properties.

Quite a number of <u>real estate investment trusts (REITs)</u> have listed securities that can be bought and sold by individuals. Incidentally, some of these may have favorable tax advantages for investors.

Real estate investments, regardless of the ownership arrangement, typically involve considerable debt leverage. The pros and cons of debt leverage are discussed in some detail in chapter 3.

Finally of course, some wealthy individuals purchase 100 percent of commercial, industrial, or multifamily residential real estate properties. The primary challenge for any but very, very wealthy investors is to achieve adequate diversification across real estate investments (see chapter 9.)

Postscript: Derivatives

The term derivative appears very often in media descriptions of sophisticated securities and transactions, but it has not yet appeared in this book. There is a reason: the term is just too broad (and therefore imprecise) to be of much use. Here is the formal definition from Investopedia's website:

"A derivative is a security whose price is determined by or derived from one or more underlying assets. The derivative itself is merely a contract between two or more parties. The most common underlying assets include stocks, bonds, commodities, currencies, interest rates, and market indexes. Most derivatives are characterized by high leverage ... Derivatives are generally used ... to hedge risk, but they can also be used for speculative purposes. For example, a European investor who purchases (some) shares of an American company on an American exchange (using U.S. dollars) would be exposed to exchange rate

<u>Real Estate Investment Trusts (REITs):</u> Corporations investing in real estate. They bear some resemblance to mutual funds, in that they are not subject to corporate tax, but unlike mutual funds they are required to distribute at least 90 percent of their income to their shareholders where they are subject to tax.

risks while holding that stock. To hedge the risk, the investor could purchase currency futures [a derivative] to lock in a specified exchange rate for the future sale and currency conversion back into Euros."

Thus, the term "derivatives" includes puts, calls, short-sale contracts, and, strictly speaking, even mutual funds.

Review Questions for Chapter 8:

1. Sketch the circumstances that might attract you to "sell short" several hundred shares of a particular corporation that you know reasonably well.
2. Using the same company as an example, might you alternatively sell a put option?
3. As an investment vehicle for your short-term savings, on what basis would you choose among a money market mutual fund, a certificate of deposit, a bank time deposit, and T-bills?
4. Describe what an "efficient market" means.
5. What are the characteristics of a corporation that would be a good target for a leveraged-buyout by a large private capital investment firm?
6. How would you go about constructing a share-price index for the U.S. pharmaceutical industry?
7. Why is a mutual fund a derivative?

Chapter Nine

PERSONAL INVESTING

Money: Like an arm or a leg—use it or lose it.

—Henry Ford

Capital: That part of wealth that is devoted to obtaining more wealth.
—Alfred Marshall

With the background knowledge gleaned from the first eight chapters, we are ready to conclude with a focus on the challenge of investing an individual's personal financial assets.

Chapter 2 reviewed the many reasons why most everyone needs to accumulate some level of savings: as a "rainy day fund" to cover unexpected emergencies; to provide the flexibility to take advantage of unexpected opportunities; for major purchases, such as a home or an extended vacation; for college and graduate school tuition and expenses for oneself or one's children; to execute a philanthropic plan; and for retirement.

Chapter 3 made it clear that the power of compound interest is the all-important reason why savings should be invested to generate income returns so that the funds will grow; they should not simply be left in a checking account or a safe-deposit box at a bank.

Chapters 6, 7, and 8 reviewed the markets—credit, equity, and other—where most savings are invested and grown.

The decisions as to which securities are optimal for a person's savings are complicated and multidimensional. It is to those decisions that we turn in this final chapter, beginning with some fundamentals.

Opportunity: A combination of the right psychological moment and some capital.
—Robert Zwickey

Pay Down Debt: An Assured Return

Only one "investment" provides an assured return: pay down your outstanding debt! This investment earns a return equivalent to the future interest payments that you have avoided. Chapter 3 discussed the advantages of debt leverage, and this observation does not nullify that discussion. Most people borrow at some times in their lives, almost always when they buy their first home. Nevertheless, many (including this author and members of his family) are uncomfortable owing money and seek to repay even mortgages, thus trading peace-of-mind for what are likely submaximum returns on their funds.

Diversification

Most investors want to avoid "putting all their eggs in one basket," even if the investment vehicle (the "basket") seems to offer high returns and acceptable risks. Unforeseen events or circumstances—and the financial world has seen plenty of these in the last several decades – may well undercut the returns and escalate the risks.

<u>Diversify</u>: Make investments across a range of opportunities; don't put all your eggs in one basket.

Accordingly, an investor should seek to <u>diversify</u> his or her investments across a broad range of security types (e.g., fixed income, corporate equities, and real estate), industry types, company sizes and maturity, and geography (domestic and global.) Reasonable diversification can be achieved even for relatively small savings amounts, as we shall see in this chapter.

Here is an example of an undiversified investment plan. A senior manager at a high-technology company has the opportunity to buy common shares of the company in advance of the company's initial public offering. She also earns common stock rights as part of her compensation package. She makes regular contributions to an IRA that is invested in the company's stock. She has great confidence in the company and is enthusiastic about its future. She has no other savings. All of her assets— her savings and her potential for future wealth, including her personal time and talent—are invested in a single company. She needs to diversify.

Another investor may be a manager at one of the many companies sponsoring a stock purchase plan for its employees. These plans typically provide some or all employees the opportunity to purchase a limited number of shares of that company, from time to time at say, a 15 percent discount from market price. While the bargain price may be too attractive to pass up, and despite the encouragement of his employer to retain shares thus acquired, he should remain alert to his need to diversify his overall investment portfolio, perhaps by selling some of his employer's shares from time to time and investing the proceeds elsewhere.

Other examples: investing all available resources in (a) stocks and none in fixed-income securities (bonds); (b) investing solely in the equities of technology-advanced companies and nothing in consumer, finance, capital equipment manufactures or other companies facing substantially less risk of technological obsolescence; (c) investing all available resources in municipal bonds offering income tax advantages but limited opportunity for capital appreciation; (d) investing solely in the securities of companies domiciled and doing all of their business in the U.S., ignoring the fact that the U.S. is increasingly dependent upon and participating in a global economy; (e) investing all available resources in U.S. government bonds because they are considered "risk free," while ignoring the risk associated with possible rapid price inflation.

In short, then, diversifying investments across several or many investment alternatives provides the investor protection against catastrophic losses. But recognize also that diversification dilutes the overall effect on wealth of a "home run" investment that delivers unusually handsome returns.

Risk Tolerance

Obviously, the need to diversify derives from the need to manage "risk." Every investor needs to think hard about personal risk tolerance: how much risk is he or she comfortable taking? The answer is not the same for each of us. The greater the investment risk accepted, the higher the probability that an extreme condition will be realized: considerable wealth or bankruptcy. For some, the possibility of bankruptcy is not particularly daunting and the opportunity for handsome gain is highly appealing; these persons have high tolerances for risk.

Not long ago, the *New Yorker* magazine ran a cartoon showing an investment manager (or perhaps he was a stockbroker) on the telephone with a client saying, "I was spreading some risk around, and apparently it all wound up in your portfolio." The implication of the cartoon—and presumably the humor therein—was that no investor would want to take on any more risk than absolutely necessary. In short, risk is to be avoided when investing.

That implication is dead wrong! Sound investing involves prudent risk-taking, not zero risk-taking. A zero-risk investment will provide a low return. Financial experts point to short-term, low-yield debt securities issued by the U.S. government as the only risk-free investment opportunity. All other investment opportunities expose the investor to some risk and, accordingly, must provide the investor the opportunity to earn a return greater than that on the U.S. government security. Otherwise, why would the investor accept the higher risk?

Thus, the reason to invest in higher-risk securities or other opportunities is to try to achieve higher return. If you are seventy-five years old with a small net worth just adequate to fund your modest retirement lifestyle, you are probably more focused on not losing money than you are on making high returns. By contrast, if you are thirty-five years old with adequate savings, a growing investment portfolio, and high-earnings years ahead of you, you might reasonably decide to diversify your investments so as to invest perhaps 25 percent of your portfolio in "higher risk/higher potential return" opportunities. If some of these risks come back to bite you, causing you to lose half of your high-risk funds, your total portfolio will have been reduced by only 12.5 percent and at your relatively young age you have ample time to rebuild that investment portfolio.

In short, risk is neither your enemy nor your friend. It is simply a fact of investing, sometimes to be avoided and sometimes to be cheerfully accepted. Be aware that an investor simply cannot and should not seek to avoid all risks.

Inflation

A risk too often overlooked by investors is that of inflation. The term inflation refers to the increase over time in a nation's price level of goods and services, and thus decreased purchasing power of the nation's money. Inflation at some level is simply a fact of life in essentially all countries and economies, developed or underdeveloped. And inflation varies year to year depending on economic and trade conditions. In general, less developed countries are subject to greater swings in inflation, but even the most developed economies suffer some fluctuations in inflation.

Deflation—decreasing prices—is also possible, but it occurs rarely, partly because government policies stress avoidance of deflation much more than avoidance of inflation, perhaps because inflation "hurts" lenders and "helps" borrowers. That is, borrowers repay their loans with inflated money—monetary units (dollars, euros, and so forth) that have decreased purchasing power. This decrease in value (or purchasing power) of each monetary unit makes the loan easier to repay. And all governments are borrowers!

Nominal vs. Real Returns

The media may report that a particular ten-year investment had a nominal return of 9 percent, but a real return of only 5 percent; that report tells us that inflation averaged four percent—the difference—over the ten-year period.

Because inflation is a nearly universal condition, nominal returns are almost universally higher than real returns. An investor might be tempted to buy a government bond issued by a Latin American country—and denominated in that country's currency—because it has a coupon rate of, say, 7 or 9 percent; that is, its nominal rate of return (assuming no defaults) is 7 or 9 percent; but if annual inflation in the issuing country averages 10 percent over the life of the bond, the real return is negative.

Nominal Return: The stated interest rate on a fixed-income security, ignoring the effects of inflation.

If you elect to keep all of your savings in bank checking accounts, and those accounts pay 1.5 percent interest per year, you are probably earning negative real returns on those savings, since inflation in the United States averages about 3 percent. Thus, the checking account is "safe" in one respect—the availability of the full value of your deposit is guaranteed by the government—but it is "unsafe" in another respect, as the deposit loses purchasing power most years. Of course, keeping your savings in the proverbial "mattress" or "sugar bowl" earns no return at all, and thus its loss of purchasing power is fully equal to the inflation rate.

Real Return: The stated interest rate on a fixed-income security, decreased or increased by the rate of inflation/deflation.

Rapidly Evolving Technology, Market, Political Risks

As a present or potential shareholder, you share with all other shareholders the operational risks of the corporation. Some of these are related to rapidly evolving technologies and changing markets. If the company operates at the frontier of engineering and scientific developments, it faces the opportunity for very rapid growth but also the threat of very rapid decline. Recall the "dot-com stock market boom and bust" that occurred for several years around the turn of the century. The excitement over new technologies and markets resulted in wholly unrealistic valuations for the shares of some high-tech companies. Unsurprisingly, many investors lost substantial sums when the "bust" caused very rapid declines in these share prices. Some of these companies failed; those that survived may never have regained their "boom" share prices.

Operational Risks: Risks that arise because of the nature of the business, competitive actions, technological changes, and actions by management.

Companies may have major exposure to political risk if they have operational units, revenues, or material sources in unstable or unpredictable foreign countries—for example, Latin America, the Middle-east, Africa, and perhaps China.

Loss of Capital and/or Income

When an investor's expectations for a company whose shares he or she owns are not realized, the share price will probably decline (or appreciate less than anticipated.) A decline may be temporary; perhaps the share price will recover before the investment is sold and the loss of capital is actually realized by the investor.

Too many investors abhor the idea of selling a stock at a price below their purchasing price; that is, they postpone or avoid a sale that will result in a capital loss. This prejudice reflects the human tendency not to admit to a mistake, in this case an investment mistake. This abhorrence is, frankly, foolish. An investor cannot change the past, and the only relevant investment question is whether to move the funds to another investment with greater potential for return or leave the funds where they are.

Occasionally, a company reduces its dividend payment to conserve cash. For example, almost all banks did so during the 2008–2009 credit crunch. Dividend cuts typically result in share price declines. This risk is most serious for those shareholders counting on regular dividend income to support their lifestyles, for example during retirement.

Volatility

We all know that the equity market as a whole moves up and down regularly—indeed daily—and these moves are widely reported, usually by reference to an "index" such as the Dow Jones Industrials Average or the Standard and Poor's 500 stock index. Some of these price movements are induced by changes in macro-economic or macro-financial changes, and some are induced by changes in investors' sentiments, perceptions, or emotions. Put another way, some market-wide price changes are rational and some are irrational. Separating the rational from the irrational is both difficult and important.

Volatility seems to be self-reinforcing. Even among professional investors, there seems to be a certain "herd instinct": what one investor does, others follow. An announcement that a certain foreign bank may default on its debt motivates investors to sell shares not only of that bank but other banks that might be affected or be next in line for default. And that action induces other investors to take similar actions. In recent years it has not been unusual to see stock markets decline by 2 percent in a single day and regain part or all of that loss on the following day.

In general, investors are well served by ignoring short-term market volatility; trying to predict short-term volatility is typically "a fool's game." Volatility is the new reality.

Investors should also remain alert for "bubbles" that build up in markets. History is replete with stories of outrageous price bubbles. The U.S. is not immune to this silliness. We had the "savings and loan bubble" of the early 1990s, the "dot-com bubble" of the early years of this century, and the "housing price bubble" of 2006–2009. Will we have other bubbles in the future? You should probably count on it.

Beta and Alpha

The term beta refers to the price volatility of a particular stock in relationship to the price volatility of the entire market. A beta of one indicates that the shares track the market in price volatility—that is, the share's volatility equals the average volatility of all shares. A beta of greater than one indicates the share's price volatility is greater than the market's overall price volatility and, of course, beta of less than one indicates the opposite.

Price volatility is neither "good" nor "bad"; it is simply a condition. Some risk-tolerant investors prefer high beta shares, believing that the volatility will provide periodic opportunities to sell the shares on the "highs" of volatility, and they are willing to wait out the "lows."

Alpha refers to changes in share prices that arise due to company operations—improvements or deteriorations—as distinguished from changes that reflect overall market volatility. The average investor need not bother trying to separate alpha from beta, but professional investors often reference this distinction.

Use of Margin

Investors seeking to leverage their investments in shares may borrow a portion of the capital they invest; they are buying on margin and most brokerage houses are prepared to provide this margin to qualified clients. Suppose the investor borrows 50 percent of the total capital deployed. As explained in chapter 4, this margin borrowing doubles the potential positive (or negative) returns on the investor's own capital, less (or plus) interest payments on the amount borrowed. Typically, the brokerage house will require the margin customer to pledge as collateral the purchased shares or other shares owned by the investor having a market value well above the amount borrowed. Should these collateral shares suffer a major decline in value such that they are now worth substantially less, the brokerage house will issue a margin call—a requirement that the investor put up additional collateral. Should the borrower be unable to do so, the brokerage house will liquidate (sell) the shares previously

Beta: Refers to the price volatility of a stock in relationship to the price volatility of the entire stock market.

Alpha: Refers to share price movements of a stock that are driven by improvements or deterioration in corporate operations and financial results, not simply from volatility.

Buying On Margin: Borrowing from the brokerage house a portion of the funds invested and secured by the investment itself; the investment is thus leveraged.

Margin Call: Will be made by the brokerage house if the market value of the securities that are the collateral for the margin loan declines to a value near the outstanding balance of the margin loan.

provided as collateral sufficient to reduce the amount of the borrowing. If margin calls are widespread across brokerage firms, these additional share sales will tend to depress stock market prices still further.

Selling Well

Most discussions of fundamentals, including the last few pages, tend to focus overwhelmingly on the what, when, and why of buying stocks. Recognize that it is as important to "sell well" as to "buy well." Don't purchase shares, put them in your bank safety deposit box and forget them, assuming they will always perform well. In the parlance of investing, when a stock ceases to be a "buy," it is generally labeled a "hold," but all "holds" should be considered candidates to sell.

Dollar-Cost Averaging

Dollar-Cost Averaging: Spreading buying or selling activity over a number of days or weeks, thereby achieving a price that will be close to the average share price for that elapsed time period.

Many investors struggle deciding on which day they should buy or sell? Maybe tomorrow will be better! They would hate to sell today and find that tomorrow the share price went up $2. One way to mitigate these concerns is to sell (or buy) over a number of trading days. Suppose you own five hundred shares of Laspa Corporation; you have become discouraged about its prospects, but you think the company might soon announce some good news. If you decide to sell one hundred shares of Laspa each week for the next five weeks, your average price per share will be the average price for the five week period. That selling (or buying) techniques is referred to as dollar-cost averaging.

"Sell Winners, Hold Losers"

Investors should periodically review their stock portfolios, looking for candidates to be sold and others where additional investment may be in order.

This review is more challenging when the investor decides he or she must pare back (reduce investments) to generate funds for other purposes, such as remodeling a home or paying tuition. At this point many investors seem to have a strong disposition to "sell winners" and "hold losers." Why? Because to sell a "loser"—an investment that lost money—requires the investor to admit to a mistake in buying the stock in the first place. Few of us eagerly admit mistakes; we are more inclined to rationalize that perhaps the "loser" will soon recover and eliminate the paper loss. In the meantime the investor sells a "winner" and smiles as he or she contemplates the capital gain realized.

The price originally paid for the "loser" is irrelevant (aside from income tax considerations.) It is what economists call a <u>sunk cost</u>, a historic fact that the investor cannot change. The "buy" or "sell" decision that the investor now faces can only affect the future, not the past. Sensible investors assess each stock position in terms of its future returns, never mind its original cost. This may lead to selling some "losers"; so be it!

> Sunk Costs:
> Historic costs
> that cannot be
> altered by any
> action taken now
> or in the future.

"Buy Low/Sell High" or "Buy High/Sell Low"

The financial markets are volatile: they can swing widely day to day, month to month, over the course of an economic cycle. Your objective is to buy low and sell high but procrastination and fear tend to push all of us in the direction of buying high and selling low. Let me explain.

Back in about the year 2000, software firms were the "hot ticket" on Wall Street, and their share prices were in some cases bid up to ridiculously high levels. The amateur investors among us almost certainly were late in recognizing these escalating prices, but once we recognized them, we were eager to get aboard this fast-moving train by buying shares. If so, we were almost certainly too late—we "bought high." When the "bust" came, many software company share prices dropped precipitously. As they fell, we amateurs were eager to minimize our losses (or get out of the stock while we still had a little appreciation in the investment.) We sold low.

When the Dow Jones Industrial Average loses 25 percent of its value, too many investors abandon all hope for stock investing and "sell out" of the market, turning all their funds into cash. That may be a smart move, but when the market begins again to move upward, many—perhaps most—of these investors remain on the sidelines, out of the market, still too fearful of its volatility. If or when they return to the market, will they be late "getting back in?" Almost certainly they will miss out on the early "comeback" of the stock market. Once again, these folks will have "sold low and bought high."

This phenomenon was documented in a recent study of twenty-year investment returns through the end of 2010. The average investor in equities earned an average of 3.83 percent per year.

The S&P 500 index posted a return of 9.14 percent over this same period, a return that could have been achieved by the average investor had she remained fully invested in a diversified set of equities for this twenty-year period.

These last few pages may convince you that you need assistance in managing your equity investments. There are plenty of professionals who can help you counteract personal emotions, predispositions, and prejudices that can too easily lead to suboptimal trading strategies.

Assistance for the Investor

The financial world is replete with individuals and companies eager to assist the individual investor, typically for a fee, in selecting appropriate investment vehicles.

Friends, relatives, work colleagues and golf partners are often full of "tips" as to what will be a "hot stock." A few of these may be useful—and may be based on more than just a guess or a hunch—but most should be ignored. Moreover, a few of these may be based on what is called "insider information"; see the discussion below.

The need for advice is strong among investors because they lack confidence—as most probably should—to select investments and time their buy and sell decisions. This eagerness for investment advice is driven both by the complexity of modern financial markets and the flood of information related to investments that is published every day—more information than the average individual investor can or has the time to digest.

But evidence abounds that so-called experts—those paid for their advice—have relatively poor track records; recall from chapter 8 both the "efficient market" hypothesis and the wide popularity of index funds. Remember too, that nobody—amateur or expert—can reliably forecast short-term movements for stock markets. Warren Buffett, the highly respected long-term investor suggests that there is no point in trying. In short, then, an investor, even with good (expensive?) advice is unlikely to be able to "time" the market.

Brokers

Brokers, typically tied to large brokerage houses such as Merrill Lynch, Morgan Stanley, A. G. Edwards, Schwab, Ameriprise, and many more, are in the business of advising clients on investments. For some, this advice runs beyond simple "stock picking" and includes a broad financial plan for the person or family, giving consideration to diversification, age of the clients, needs for cash now and in the future, and estate plans. Brokers are required to have quite extensive training before they are permitted to "practice." And their performance is closely monitored by their employer, by the stock exchanges, and by the Securities and Exchange Commission to assure that they know their customers well enough to be assured that the investments recommended are appropriate for them. Brokers do not, however, have a fiduciary responsibility to place the best interests of their clients ahead of their own business interests.

Brokers do some of their own investigation of individual companies but they also rely on information and suggestions fed to them by the securities research teams at their home offices. Brokerage firms also effect the transactions in ways that are meant to be advantageous to their clients. In recent years the fees charged for executing a "buy" or "sell" order have been reduced very substantially; for example, Schwab now charges less than $10 per transaction. These reduced fees have resulted in huge increases in the volume of transactions.

Mutual Funds

Chapter 8 discussed the mutual fund industry in some depth. These firms provide to individual investors, at relatively low cost, research expertise, transaction efficiency, and broad diversification. They have a fiduciary responsibility to their investors.

Investment Firms, Wealth Management Firms, Bank Trust Departments

Finally, the business of a large number of investment firms in this country is to help individuals, families, and institutions to manage their invested capital (again, of course, for a fee). Some of these firms focus just on stocks and bonds; others consider a broader array of investment opportunities and strategies. Trust companies (including trust departments of commercial banks) assist wealthy individuals and families with estate planning, including passing assets on to subsequent generations, minimizing estate taxes and probate fees, and effecting philanthropic plans of the deceased. The clientele of some of these firms is limited to those with great wealth—say, in excess of $100 million. But some competent investment firms are willing to accept clients (or families) with investible wealth of, say, $2,000,000 (I know that sounds like a lot to some of us!)

Employees of mutual funds and investment firms do have a fiduciary responsibility to look out for the best interests of their clients. For example, they are not permitted to buy and sell shares for their own personal accounts (in order to take advantage of better prices) in advance of trades on behalf of their clients.

Securities Analysts

All of these companies that provide assistance to the investor employ securities analysts. The job of these analysts is to ferret out companies that appear to represent good investment opportunities, and also to discern as early as possible companies whose fortunes are fading and thus whose stocks should perhaps be sold.

The analysts' work involves reading published information about a particular company, its competitors, the industry or industries in which it participates, and economic conditions that may benefit or hurt the company's profitability. Analysts also may meet with the company's management to better understand the company's present condition and strategic changes (including new technologies, products, and markets) that the company may be contemplating. Some of these analysts become quite expert on the industries they follow most closely. These buy-side analysts work for mutual funds and other investment firms. The analysts' recommendations are retained within these firms and inform their buy and sell decisions.

Sell-side analysts work for brokerage firms. They are an important source of information that the brokers share with their clients in helping them to make buy and sell decisions.

Insider Trading

Insider Trading: Involves making a buy or sell decision based upon information obtained from so-called insiders and thus not available to the investing public.

Insider Information: All information known only to individuals or firms that have access to privileged (confidential) company information that is not available to the investing public.

A distressing number of prominent and wealthy financial executives have gone to jail in recent years for the crime of insider trading. To understand this crime, consider first the definition of an inside trader: an individual who uses information about a particular company to trade in its securities—either buying or selling—before that information is disclosed by the company to the investing public at large. Such information might relate to, for example, a merger being negotiated, a key executive or director joining or leaving the company, a pending decision by the board to repurchase the company's common stock, a pending decision by the board to sell additional common equity, a pending investigation of the company or one of its key persons by a federal regulator or law officer, or financial results about to be released.

Who are insiders? Insiders are those who have access to confidential corporate information. Certainly all corporate officers and directors, including the director of accounting, the executive assistants to the chief executive and the chief financial officers, and many others (but certainly not all company employees) are insiders.

There are no bright lines that define who qualifies as an insider and what qualifies as insider information that might affect trading in, and thus the market price of, the company's stock. Regulators and prosecutors generally have the benefit of hindsight about actual stock price movements, and they can determine exactly who has bought or sold shares in the particular company and thereby benefited illegally from insider information. Accordingly, they have quite solid evidence when they decide to indict or bring other action against insiders.

If an insider (sometimes referred to as the "tipper") tells an outsider (the "tippee") a piece of inside information, that outsider thereby becomes an insider and is prohibited from buying or selling that company's shares until the information is made public. So to avoid becoming a tippee, be careful what you hear!

To make the matter even more complex, an outsider is not precluded from seeking and finding—or just stumbling across—important information about a company and, based on that information, trading in its stock. For example, suppose a long-time investor in Company A drives by the plant parking lot and finds many fewer cars than were there a few months earlier. She may surmise that the company is laying off employees; earnings and the stock price are likely to decline in the near term, and thus, she should sell her stock. Or suppose a potential investor concludes after independent study but no "tips," that Company B would be a very attractive acquisition candidate (at a premium share price) for Large Company C. He is free to acquire shares in Company B.

Traders vs. Investors

One cannot usefully generalize on such matters as (a) how long a person should hold a particular stock or bond, (b) whether a person should sell the stock if it goes up or down a certain percentage, (c) whether a person is better off buying high price/earnings ratio stocks or ones with low P/E's, (d) whether one's investments in bonds should be limited to AAA-rated bonds or whether buying lower rated bonds might provide both higher current return and also the opportunity for capital appreciation (see chapter 7.)

Nonetheless, history suggests that, for the nonprofessional investor, investment performance will be better if the investor takes the long view and refrains from doing a great deal of trading: chasing the latest hot deal or overreacting to market volatility. By the time you read about a "hot stock" in the general or financial press, its price has probably already climbed significantly, a price rise that you didn't and won't participate in if you buy now. Remember, when you buy a stock or bond, you are buying its future, not its past.

Moreover, bear in mind that whenever you buy shares in a particular company, the seller on the other side of the transaction (your counterparty) is selling those shares. As you are optimistic that the price of your acquired shares will rise, your counterparty is confident of the opposite.

Kahneman, the Nobelist economist quoted earlier, asks, "Why do investors, both amateur and professional, stubbornly believe that they can do better than the [overall] market, contrary to economic theory that *most of them accept*, and contrary to what they could learn from a dispassionate evaluation of their personal experience?" He also notes that on average the most active traders had the poorest results, while the investors who traded least had the best results.

Comparing Investment Returns

A common mistake made by investors is assessing their returns on investment over too short a time period. Or worse, deciding to shift their funds to investment vehicles that most recently have had the best results.

Morningstar and other reporting services award "stars" to certain mutual funds with the highest returns over the past three or six months. These stellar short-term results are as likely to arise from "good luck" as from "good stock picking." Companies and industries come in and out of favor among investors (including professional investors) and analysts.

During the meltdown of the home mortgage credit market, one smart investor made billions of dollars for himself and his clients in the years 2006–2009. The result: new clients flocked to his firm to manage their money. In the first three quarters of 2011, his firm incurred losses of about 50 percent of the funds entrusted to it.

Also, note that this same investor has to achieve a 100 percent increase in value—a doubling—in order to return his fund to its late 2010 value. Many of us lose sight of the fact that a 25 percent price decline—from, say, $100 to $75—is not recouped by a subsequent 25 percent gain; instead it takes a 33 percent ($25 is one-third of $75) gain to recoup the loss.

Investors are wise to look at their own investment performance (or that of their investment advisors) over short-term periods (say, one year), intermediate-term periods (say, three and five years), and long-term periods (for example, ten years and beyond). Investors can run into lucky streaks or rough patches, all of which may be revealed by looking at these different time periods.

Before you get discouraged, remember that the U.S. stock market over the great sweep of time—say, over more than 100 years—has delivered returns averaging between 8 and 9 percent per year. But these returns have been anything but consistent! Consider the Great Depression, 1929 until the late 1930s. Think about the prosperous period following the conclusion of World War II; the stock-price stagnation of the 1970s, the so-called dot-com boom and bust at the turn of this century; and, more recently, the Great Recession from about 2007 through at least 2011.

The calculated, annualized growth rate of a portfolio (yours or a mutual fund's) for a lengthy period can be much affected by the choice of beginning and ending year. Here is a simple example. Suppose a particular mutual fund had a net asset value (NAV) at the end of 2014 of $51.37 and an NAV of $34.71 at the end of 2004, ten years earlier. For the ten years, its performance was an average annual price gain of 4 percent (ignoring any dividends paid, which would improve the calculated performance.) The next year, 2015, the fund reports a year-end value of $52.91, a 3.0 percent gain from 2014, but a ten-year average annual return of 7.5 percent. How could the ten-year performance grow so handsomely when in fact the one-year (2015) return was only 3.0 percent? Here are the NAVs in tabular form:

Year-End	NAV
2004	$34.71
2005	$26.03
-----	-----
2014	$51.37
2015	$52.91

What changed was the beginning year of the ten-year period, now 2005, not 2004. In 2005, a bear-market year, this fund lost 25 percent of its NAV. So starting the ten-year calculation from that point, the annualized return for the ten-year period was indeed 7.5 percent. The moral of the story: in calculating a multiyear return, be careful to choose an appropriate starting year.

Assessments of investment performances for portfolios and mutual funds are typically assessed by comparing them with relevant benchmarks, for a single year or multiple years. These benchmarks are chosen to reflect both the composition of the portfolio and its long-term return objective(s). If your portfolio (or your mutual fund's portfolio) consists dominantly of large industrial companies headquartered in the US, then the Dow Jones' and Standard and Poor's indices are relevant benchmarks, but so also is the performance of competing mutual funds. If your portfolio is heavily weighted toward smaller, growth stocks, the NASDAQ index may be the relevant benchmark. If your portfolio consists of both stocks and bonds, you will probably want to use two benchmarks or a blend of two or more.

Benchmark: Typically an average of other portfolios (for example, mutual funds) that have the same investment objectives, or an index that resembles the composition of the portfolio being assessed.

Income Tax Considerations

This book has had relatively little to say about personal income taxes and their impact on an individual's financial decision-making. One reason is that the income tax laws change with great frequency in this country. Another is my personal view that financial decisions made primarily to seek income tax advantages are very often unwise.

Passive Income: Includes interest and dividends payments received by a taxpayer.

Earned Income: The taxpayer's earnings in the form of salary and wages.

Cost Basis: The cost basis of an investment is typically the acquisition price of that investment.

What can usefully be said is that your investment decisions will typically expose you to two kinds of taxes: taxes on income earned from the investments (i.e., interest and dividend receipts), and taxes on capital gains and possibly tax savings on capital losses. A reminder: interest and dividend payments received (often called passive income) are taxed, just as your salary (earned income) is. Income tax rates on passive income are not always the same as income tax rates on earned income. Income taxes in the US are "graduated," which means that, generally, the higher your income, the greater the percentage of your income (not simply the total tax dollars) you will be required to pay.

A capital gain, in short, is earned when you sell one of your investments at a price higher than its acquisition (purchase) price, referred to as your cost basis. That amount is then taxable according to a separate schedule of tax rates: capital gains rates. Importantly, only "net capital gains"—gains net of losses—are taxed. If capital losses exceed capital gains, those losses may serve to reduce the individual's income taxes against ordinary income this year (or, under certain circumstances, in a past or future year).

As an aside for those fortunate enough to have been given or have inherited securities: the cost basis of an asset received as a gift is the cost basis of the donor; the cost basis of an asset received by bequest is its market value at the date of death of the person who made the bequest. Understandably then, the gifting of very low-basis assets is often delayed until death so as to obtain the cost-basis step-up for the inheritor of the asset.

Remember that when an opportunity presents itself to postpone the payment of taxes to a later year, that postponement represents savings because you can invest those "postponed tax payments" to earn additional income until the tax is ultimately paid. Here's an example: suppose in a particular tax year you have accumulated substantial capital gains on which you will be required to pay capital gains tax. However, your portfolio also includes a number of investment positions with current market value well below what you paid for them. They present an opportunity for you to "harvest" capital losses that can offset some or all of the gains you realized earlier in the year, thus reducing your tax payments for the current year; you have postponed some of the capital gains tax, but you haven't eliminated it.

Suppose you anticipate that these "losing" investments will soon increase in price, and thus, you are reluctant to liquidate them. You could sell the positions now, record the capital losses, and repurchase the positions later. (But caution: you must not repurchase them within thirty days from the date you sell.)

As the end of the tax year approaches, investors should carefully review their investment positions to determine what sales or purchases might defer tax payments to future years.

Some Concluding Thoughts

A popular theme among regulators, observers, and critics of investment and other markets is the need for greater transparency: greater clarity regarding particular transactions as well as the mechanics of the organized marketplaces. It's hard to make a reasonable argument against greater transparency, but it is also difficult to achieve transparency in a rational way. All too often, the demand for greater transparency gets translated into strident calls for greater disclosure. But more disclosure in turn has three problems:

Transparency: Refers to the extent to which disclosed information about a contract or transaction provides full disclosure to the counterparty.

1. It ought not reveal inappropriate personal information about (that is, invade the privacy rights of) employees and directors, or comprise the company's competitive position by revealing confidential information pertinent to that competition.
2. The disclosure documents are drafted by lawyers with the primary aim of providing maximum protection of their clients from liability; the layperson has difficulty interpreting the resulting "legalese."
3. Disclosure documents can become so lengthy that many of us are disinclined to even read them, to say nothing of study and really comprehend them. How often have you read carefully, and fully comprehended— in advance of signing—the disclosure documents that

are legally required to accompany (a) consumer credit card applications, (b) rental car contracts, (c) hotel registration forms, (d) auto loan agreements, (e) medical service agreements, (f) the seller's disclosure documents when buying real estate, and so on?

Bear in mind that our lives are full of actual or potential conflicts of interest. Be cautious—maybe even politely suspicious—but not to the point of paranoia. After all, every buyer-and-seller pair has a conflict of interest as to price, although not in the desire to conclude the transaction.

A stockbroker may be more eager to sell you securities that are already held in his firm's inventory because his commission may be greater than if he effected the transaction in the open market. Similarly, a broker may find it personally advantageous to sell you a mutual fund managed by her employer rather than one managed by a third party; can you count on the broker providing you unbiased advice? An auto dealer may strongly urge you to finance your purchase through credit source M. Source M may be in the dealer's best interest but not the auto buyer's. A little persistent questioning early in any of these negotiations will generally uncover any latent conflicts of interest. For example, who is the counterparty of the transaction she is recommending, or what commission or rebate will the auto dealer earn from lender M and lender P? As the old saying goes, "Follow the money!"

Review Questions for Chapter 9:

1. What are the alternative ways that an investor with limited funds to invest in equities can achieve sufficient diversification?
2. Suppose that you have only moderate tolerance for investment risk. Would you split your investment funds among three "pools," low-risk, medium-risk, and high-risk securities, or would you put all your funds in the medium-risk pool?
3. In the period 2010–2011, interest rates paid on bank deposits, CDs, and government notes and bonds were very low, generally lower than the rate of inflation (which itself was around 2.5 percent). Why would people be willing to earn "negative real return" by putting their savings and/or investments in these accounts/securities?
4. Why do you think price volatility in the stock market has been and continues to be quite high?
5. How does personal emotion affect people's decision to buy or sell shares in a particular company when the market over the previous three months declined by about 20 percent? How do you think you would react?
6. Explain the difference in relationship between a stockbroker and her client and an investment advisor and his client.
7. Quite a number of wealthy, intelligent people have in recent years been found guilty of insider training and sentenced to prison terms. How can we explain this spate of illegal actions?

8. Late in the year, why might an investor with a sizeable investment portfolio sell a number of positions that result in losses?

9. Consider examples from your own experience where an emphasis on full disclosure has resulted in such a lengthy and convoluted disclosure document that you decided not to read it.

Afterword

Perhaps a book of this sort should conclude with pithy advice to the reader from the author. I prefer to do as I have done throughout the book: turn to quotes from wise people down through the ages.

The winds and waves are always on the side of the ablest navigators.
—Edward Gibbon

Nothing great is created suddenly, any more than a bunch of grapes or a fig. If you tell me you desire a fig, I answer you that there must be time. Let it first blossom, then bear fruit, then ripen.

—Epictetus

Only those who dare to fail greatly can ever achieve greatly.
—Robert F. Kennedy

Do what you can, with what you have, where you are.
—Theodore Roosevelt

Good is not good, where better is expected.
—Thomas Fuller

He that leaveth nothing to Chance will do few things ill, but he will do very few things.
—George, Lord Halifax

There is nothing so useless as doing efficiently that which should not be done.
—Peter Drucker

Riches: Not the end, but only a change in worries.
—Epicurus

I'm so happy to be rich, I'm willing to take all of the consequences.
—Howard Ahmanson

I am easily satisfied with the very best.
—Winston Churchill

Progress: To act, that each tomorrow finds us further than today.
—Henry Wadsworth Longfellow

Index